ENDOR

"Sandra offers extremely practical tools and perspectives for anyone facing a loss of any size. The power of her insights are rooted in her extraordinary journey of loss and recovery - an incredible personal story that will touch and inspire any reader."

—Jonathan Ellerby, PhD, CEO, TAO
Inspired Living and Best-selling author of
Inspiration Deficit Disorder and **Return To The Sacred**

"It is said that the best teacher is one who has experienced what they teach. In this book, Sandra shares her stories of loss and shares exercises and techniques she learned and has used to overcome the grief and loss she has experienced. She weaves together skillfully the power of forgiveness and surrender, consciousness, energy, chakras, and her skills as a Feng Shui practitioner to offer a holistic way to heal grief and loss."

—Carol Ritberger, Ph.D.,
Medical Intuitive and Best-selling author of
Healing Happens with Your Help and Your Personality Your Health

TESTIMONIALS

"Sandra is a bright, shining star who easily guides you towards the life you desire. Her optimistic spirit and understanding of life's challenges provided a safe place where I easily opened to change. Her kindness and wisdom of body, mind and spirit are solid. I love all the tools she incorporates and has to choose from, it is a rare person with so many dynamic skills. Thank you, Sandra, for your positive influence on my life."

—Betsy, RN, HTP, CH,
Portland, OR

"I was referred to Sandra after my divorce to help me pick up the pieces of my life and start new again. I had no idea what I wanted to create until I worked with Sandra. She coached me step-by-step towards my desires. Amazing things started happening in my life when I was able to clear the blocks and move forward. I highly recommend Sandra to anyone who is seeking clarity and direction in their life after divorce. Thank you Sandra!"

—Karen,
Network Marketing Consultant,
Phoenix, AZ

"Sandra, I can't begin to thank you for your wonderful Grief Relief Retreat, *Unlocking the Grief Code*. I didn't think that I was dealing with that much grief and wasn't sure if I actually *needed* to attend. I am so grateful that I made the choice to participate. The way you explained the various layers of grief was indeed eye opening as you connected the mind, body and soul. The steps and tools that you introduced to address those layers were magical. Your guest speakers added so much to the healing process, and my gratitude journal is next to my night stand. Thank you!"

—CK Duncan,
Reiki Master and Author of
A Love Child's Journey,
Rocklin, CA

"During my experience at the Grief Recovery Retreat with Sandra Ruggles, I have been able to release what no longer serves my highest good. I received insight and clarity through forgiveness towards others as well as forgiveness of myself. We all have endured a loss at some point in our lives. Sometimes it's a loss through death and sometimes it can be a loss of self. Sandra has shown me that love is greater and stronger than any form of loss. Releasing what no longer serves me has opened a Divine flow of goodness that is no longer obstructed by grief. Let go and let the love in!"

—Sarah Cheplick,
Spiritual Life Coach, Placerville, CA

Unlocking the GRIEF CODE

Unlocking the GRIEF CODE

A Grief Recovery Manual
Using Mind, Body & Spirit
Healing "Soul"utions

SANDRA RUGGLES

BALBOA
PRESS
A DIVISION OF HAY HOUSE

Copyright © 2013 Sandra Ruggles.

All rights reserved. No part of this book may be used or reproduced by any means, graphic, electronic, or mechanical, including photocopying, recording, taping or by any information storage retrieval system without the written permission of the publisher except in the case of brief quotations embodied in critical articles and reviews.

Balboa Press books may be ordered through booksellers or by contacting:

Balboa Press
A Division of Hay House
1663 Liberty Drive
Bloomington, IN 47403
www.balboapress.com
1-(877) 407-4847

Because of the dynamic nature of the Internet, any web addresses or links contained in this book may have changed since publication and may no longer be valid. The views expressed in this work are solely those of the author and do not necessarily reflect the views of the publisher, and the publisher hereby disclaims any responsibility for them.

The author of this book does not dispense medical advice or prescribe the use of any technique as a form of treatment for physical, emotional, or medical problems without the advice of a physician, either directly or indirectly. The intent of the author is only to offer information of a general nature to help you in your quest for emotional and spiritual well-being. In the event you use any of the information in this book for yourself, which is your constitutional right, the author and the publisher assume no responsibility for your actions.

Any people depicted in stock imagery provided by Thinkstock are models, and such images are being used for illustrative purposes only.
Certain stock imagery © Thinkstock.

Printed in the United States of America

ISBN: 978-1-4525-6709-9 (sc)
ISBN: 978-1-4525-6711-2 (hc)
ISBN: 978-1-4525-6710-5 (e)

Library of Congress Control Number: 2013901908

Balboa Press rev. date: 3/6/2013

I dedicate this book

to my Dad

Fred Beck

and

my two children

Adam Ruggles and Rhonda Claycomb

and

my four grandchildren

Emma, Aiden, Kaela and Amber

and to my fifth grandchild

who is coming into this world in August

They are the greatest joys in my life!

I've written this book in memory of my

First husband Duane Peter Ruggles

And

My mother Gemma Beck

With Love and Blessings

TABLE OF CONTENTS

Foreword . . . . *xi*
Acknowledgments . . . . *xv*
Introduction . . . . *xix*

Chapter 1	My Grief Story	1
Chapter 2	No More Victim Consciousness	9
Chapter 3	The Healing Power Of Forgiveness	16
Chapter 4	The Shift Of Consciousness	24
Chapter 5	Unlocking The Grief Code – Healing For The Mind.	35
Chapter 6	Unlocking The Grief Code – Healing For The Divine Physical Body	51
Chapter 7	Unlocking The Grief Code – Aligning With Spirit For Healing.	74
Chapter 8	Your New Beginning – Your Roadmap To Wholeness	90
Chapter 9	Your Purpose, Passion & Pleasure Map	103
Chapter 10	The Tao Of Healing Using Feng Shui Principles For Grief And Loss	110

Conclusion 137
Author Biography 141
$100 Bonus Gift Included! 143

Foreword

By Carol Ritberger PhD

We all have, or will, experience the loss of someone or something we love, and each of us will deal with it differently, because dealing with loss and grief isn't a one-size-fits all. My story of grief and the change maker in my life was the loss of a granddaughter who lived for only six short days. Yet, in that short expanse of time, all of the lives she touched would become changed forever. And even to this day, they're still being changed. I married a wonderful man with two children and it was his daughter who presented us with this beautiful granddaughter. His family was not like mine in the sense that they didn't talk about how they felt, nor would they verbalize to each other how much they loved and cared for each other. Their focus was more on the mechanics of being a family rather than living and loving as a family. However, that changed the day Stephani died.

In honor of her short time gracing this earth, we as a family decided to change the way we interacted. We decided to forgive and to heal the past by each of us writing letters to each other about how much we loved each other and what we found special about the day and what we appreciated. In the time of grief, having something to do that has meaning is an important part of the healing process. So, each day we wrote about what we loved about that day, what we loved about the times we shared together, and what we loved about being a family. Then every day we would mail these letters to each other. We did this for a month and each day and each letter seemed to miraculously heal the grief that we all felt, while at the same time, creating a loving bond that only a family can offer. But the story doesn't end there. One year after Stephani's death, my husband and I were invited to a memorial service offered by the hospital where she died to share our letters with other families who lost their children and grandchildren. It seems our little angel was still doing her work and touching the lives of so many people who were working through their own grief.

When we experience grief, we run through a gamut of emotions and times that seem dark and daunting. Yet, it's through those tough times that we learn the most about who we are and what we're capable of handling. We learn the importance of forgiving and how important it is for us to shift our perceptions and expand our consciousness so we can see situations and experiences differently.

The gift of loss is that it reminds us of how precious life is and how each day, each experience, and each relationship has meaning and purpose. The gift of grief is that it allows us to connect deeply with our emotional nature so we can use our emotions as healing tools—tools that can move us into a state of grace where we can discover our purpose, find our passion, and experience pleasure doing things that are important to us. The gift of this book is that it looks holistically at loss and grief, and offers you the reader, the opportunity to see yourself differently, to view your life differently, and to heal in a different and more spiritual way. Its words encourage and inspire, and provide the tools needed to create your own roadmap to wholeness where every day is a new beginning and the beginning of a new life.

It is said that the best teacher is one who has experienced what they teach. In this book, Sandra shares her stories of loss and shares exercises and techniques she learned and has used to overcome the grief and loss she has experienced. She weaves together skillfully the power of forgiveness and surrender, consciousness, energy, chakras, and her skills as a Feng Shui practitioner to offer a holistic way to heal grief and loss. I've known Sandra for many years and had the pleasure of having her as a student in my mind/body/energy healing class and what struck me the most about her was her compassionate nature and her tireless desire to help other people in their healing. And here she is again, doing what she does best, helping people heal through the words and thoughts she shares in her book, *Unlocking the Grief Code*. Well done, Sandra. I have no doubt that your healing work including the writing of this book is part of your divine plan and is why you so bravely faced the challenges that life placed before you.

Carol Ritberger, Ph.D. –
Author of Healing Happens With Your Help

Acknowledgments

It has been quite a journey writing this book the last year and a half. I've had this book in my mind for over a decade, but never quite ready to write it until two years ago. Writing this book was very healing for me.

There are so many that helped guide me towards the completion of this book. I must include these individuals because this book would not have been written without each and every one of them.

I would like to begin with my ultimate coach and best friend in the world Yessica Alaya from the Netherlands. It was Yessica that coached me to completing the book each and every day for the last year. When I would get frustrated and unfocused, it was Yessica who would coach me back to focus and keep me on target to finish the book. A big thanks to Yessica for helping me edit the book at the completion stage. I am so thankful and grateful for all the time Yessica put into helping me complete this book. I could not have completed this book without her.

The next person who I want to thank is my best friend in Sacramento, California, Colleen Duncan. Colleen spent countless hours with me talking about my book, giving me advice and coaching me to write and finish this book. Colleen is a published author herself and her advice and knowledge about writing a book was absolutely necessary as I started down the path as a new author to the finish line. A great big thank you to Colleen for all those hours spent with me the last 2 years. I could not have done this without your help and advice.

Next, I would like to thank Connie Vaughn for contributing her Affirmative Prayers for Surrender, Acceptance and Forgiveness. Connie and I have been great friends for the past 9 years and she has a gift for writing the most effective Affirmative Prayers I've ever seen. I am so thankful and grateful to Connie for allowing me to use her prayers in my book to share with the world.

A special thanks to all my teachers over the years, especially Carol Ritberger, Ph.D. for reading my book and writing the Foreword. A special thank you to Jonathan Ellerby, Ph.D. who took the time to read my book and provide me with a glowing endorsement.

Additionally, I would like to thank my editor and friend, Andrea Glass for editing my book quickly and efficiently. I would like to thank the staff at Balboa Press for always being there to answer my every question about the publishing process and encouraging me along the way.

A special thanks to all of my family and friends who have supported the writing of this book. I am so thankful and grateful to each and every one of you.

In grateful honor of the late Debbie Ford who was the shining light example and role model for me the last 7 years. I had the honor to travel with Debbie in 2006 to Venice, Italy, Turkey, and the Greek Islands studying with her and her coaches. In October 2012, I had the blessing of traveling with Debbie to Egypt, Israel, Greece, Rome and the Amalfi Coast visiting all the Holy Lands and be in her heartwarming presence.

In grateful appreciation of Marianne Williamson who inspired me to finish my book 'when the completion got tough' based on her confidence expressed in her books and her presence.

And last but not least, I want to thank God, the Angels, the Ascended

Masters, the Ancestors and Spirit Guides for their contribution to the book. While writing this book, it was clear that the Divine Presence of these Angelic Beings were channeling this information through me to those who need to hear the message of healing grief. I am so thankful and grateful and I say

    Thank you, Thank you, Thank you!

Introduction

Most people who pick up this book, have been attracted to it because they are going through a loss and maybe this is you. The truth is that we all face loss, no matter who we are or what life story we carry. Loss is a part of life. We face losses of all kinds during our life and each and every day is filled with little losses and disappointments that add up if we don't have the right tools or insight to cope. In many ways, this is a book for everyone. However, on the other hand, you may now be experiencing grief and loss so much so that you don't know what to do to release the mental, physical, emotional, social or spiritual suffering and find relief. You may be caught up in the vicious cycle of pain, and you don't know how to move forward towards living a life free from the deep intense sorrow or loss. Grief is an intense feeling caused by the disruption of a familiar pattern in life. It's about change of the familiar to the unfamiliar. For those of us who have experienced it, it's a heaviness that isn't easily lifted and can affect every part of life. Those who surround you during this time sometimes don't understand what you're going through and this can make it even more difficult. As a society we haven't been taught that grief is a normal reaction to loss. As a result, others don't understand how to help or know what to say—which can make life even more uncomfortable.

This book is designed to help you recover from your grief. It's a guide to help you take the necessary action steps to regain your overall well-being and become a whole person again. The first chapter is about my grief story and offers information relating to where you may be right now.

You must understand where you are at present to know where you're going next. In chapters 5 through 7, you'll learn the mind, body and spirit healing "soul"utions to give you powerful tools and techniques to incorporate into your life to be happy and at peace. After you learn the tools and techniques for happiness and the pathway to a peaceful heart, chapters 8 through 10 will help you create and implement a roadmap to a new beginning and a life you'll love.

By the time you're done reading this book, you'll have learned new ways to live your life free from the deep suffering and grief you're experiencing now. You'll have a detailed life plan to build an abundant and prosperous life ahead of you. It's my wish for all of you reading this book that you heal easily, effortlessly and faster than you ever imagined.

Why am I writing this book? To help others heal their emotional pain and grief as I've healed and will continue to heal mine. I am starting this book at the beginning of my life at 2 days old when I was given up for adoption by my birth mother. However, another ending has occurred in my life right now as I write this book. It is 5 days after my divorce has been finalized by the court. I'm now single. This is the new beginning of the end of a 12-year marriage and a 17-year relationship with a man I now call my ex-husband. So in chapter 1, you'll find my entire grief story over the course of my 53 years on this planet and you will understand why I decided to write this book.

If you've been on the divorce path, you know that even if it's the right thing to do, it's a significant loss resulting in grief and feelings of failure. I gave the marriage everything I had for 12 years until I woke up at 50 and I realized I deserved to be happy. I hadn't been really happy in the last 10 years from when I left the marriage the first time. I had left my marriage 3 different times and returned trying to make it work each time for one more time. I'd tell myself maybe this time it would be different. If I could just work on myself and become a better me, he would love me and things would be different. I did work on myself, but to my surprise, I found the self-love that had been missing all those years and decided to change my life. I decided I would incorporate into my life the things

I loved without the approval of anyone else in my sphere of friends and family. I lost family members and friends who didn't understand me and what I was going through during my grief, but then I gained new family and friends who accepted me for who I was and who I was becoming. I began the journey that would take many years of self-discovery in a quest for happiness, love and joy. The end result of my journey is the catalyst for this book where I take you step by step through my life and what has helped me to heal the pain, suffering, anger, chaos, heartbreak, grief and loss in my life.

Why am I qualified to write this book? I will tell you that I don't have any degrees in psychology or psychotherapy. Yet, I'm qualified to write this book because I've lived it. I've felt the emotions of grief and loss firsthand and have reinvented my life not once, but 3 times due to the death of a spouse, divorce and family estrangements. I will tell you that I do have two degrees, but not in psychology. I graduated in 1991 with a Bachelor of Science in Business Administration with a concentration in Real Estate and Land Use from California State University, Sacramento. In 2005, I received a Ph.D. in Esoteric Philosophy from the Ritberger Institute in California after studying with Carol Ritberger, Medical Intuitive, for 5 years. In 2007, I was Certified as a Master Results Life and Business Coach with Five International Certifications in Master Results Coaching, Leadership, Hypnosis and Neuro Linguistic Programming. In addition, I studied at the Grief Coach Academy in Los Angeles in 2011 to receive specialized training in Grief Recovery Coaching. In 2011, I also completed my first year as a Science of Mind Practitioner which includes Spiritual Coaching.

I've been in Real Estate most of my adult life in conjunction with being a Holistic Practitioner. In 1997, I studied the Art and Science of Feng Shui and became Certified in the Black Hat Tantric Buddhism Method in 2000. I loved using Feng Shui to help my friends and family and for my Real Estate business, so I started a Feng Shui Design business in the year 2000 doing home and business consultations as well as teaching it. I wanted to learn more, and in 2004, I attended the Golden

Gate School of Feng Shui in San Francisco and studied Classical Feng Shui. I enhanced my business to include Classical Feng Shui and the Four Pillars of Destiny Chinese Astrology with my consultations. I'm a perpetual student as you can see, yet through all this study, I was gathering healing tools and techniques to heal myself from the grief and loss I had experienced while helping others heal their lives. So, I believe this is what gives me the qualifications to write this book.

You will learn first-hand how to heal your mind, body and spirit in ways uniquely mapped for you. You will learn from me, someone who has been there through the emotional pain, the grief and the struggles—and has used these healing "soul"utions to climb out of the vicious cycle of the emotional pain and grief to live a life of happiness and peace of mind.

Even though this book is being written at a pivotal ending in my life, I'm at the beginning of my new life. Through the love of God in and through myself and those who have supported me in my growth and evolutionary process, I'm blessed to write this book with the hope of helping all who read it with a new beginning of life after loss and grief.

Chapter 1

My Grief Story

"I trust the eternalness of life and know that loved ones who have passed on, still live on. It is in this awareness I dicover comfort, and for this I am grateful"

—*Daily Word*

I WAS BORN INTO GRIEF IN July of 1959 in Syracuse, New York. My mother was unmarried and 18 years old when she gave birth to me. It was unheard of in 1959 for a woman to have a baby out of wedlock and keep it, so my mother gave me up for adoption. It would disgrace the entire family if she were to keep me and try to raise me as a single parent. Two days later, my mother would drive to Rochester, New York with the social worker and place me in the Foster Care system.

I consider myself one of the lucky adoptees. After my birth, my mother named me Theresa Marie after Saint Theresa of Avila. I actually was given a name which is more than what most other adoptees I've met have had. Before she placed me into the Foster Care system, she pinned two medals to my tiny body. One was of Saint Theresa, and the other was the Divine Mother Mary which would be my protectors as I began my new adopted life. These medals along with a little yellow blanket was all I took with me at 2 days old to a foster home that was as foreign to me as being on the planet earth. The abandonment, grief and loss of my mother began at 2 days old.

I lived in the foster home for a little more than 3 months. I have a letter written by the foster care mother who took care of me during that time. She included my habits, my schedule and some history on the way I was cared for. She noted that I wasn't called a name during that time and only picked up and held at certain times of the day. A very strict schedule was followed for food, baths and sleep with minimal intimacy. A child born to its mother who stays with its mother never feels this separation from mother and the familiar, safe surroundings and familiar smells and voices.

Never quite feeling these comforting and familiar surroundings creates an immediate crisis and trauma for the adopted child. I believe our adoption system should be changed to give a birth mother and child a chance to be together for at least 8 weeks and then slowly integrate the adoptive parents into the child's life. This would give the biological mother time and opportunity to make an informed decision about relinquishing her baby, a decision which would affect her and her child for the rest of their lives. It would give the adopted baby time to have the comfort and support of the familiar mother who carried the child for 9 months. After 8 weeks, the baby would feel safe and supported, and the slow transition to the adoptive mother could be made in a less traumatizing way to the baby. The birth mother would have time to heal her body, emotions and mind as she relinquished her child with certainty. In the animal world, we don't remove offspring from the mother for 6 to 8 weeks or the offspring may die. This leads me to ask the question: *Why do we do that to human babies?*

I was adopted by a good German/Italian family on November 5th, 1959. Again, I was one of the lucky ones who had found a home with a mother and father. I was told early on at the age of 5 years old that I was, "picked from all the other babies in the nursery" because I was a special child.

When I was told that I was adopted at 5 years old, the only thing I remember thinking is, I'm different somehow. I did look different than the rest of my family, so I believed I was a child who was special but different. I began to see the differences more than the similarities as I tried to fit in and play the role of the chameleon adoptee who can fit into any surrounding. However, by playing that role, it was the beginning of losing myself and who I really was in the process at a time in a child's life when it's so important to know the truth of who you are. As a child, I tried to please everyone around me; then in entering the adolescent years, I started to rebel as a teenager.

There are two types of adoptees: the good adoptee and the bad adoptee. I was the rebel who was in search of myself at any cost and doing it my way. Therefore, I was the "bad" adoptee. I ran away from home, skipped school on a regular basis and my friends became my family of choice. That is until I met the love of my life at 15. During this time, I would learn that the only mother I had ever known had breast cancer. These two events would change my life forever.

This was the perfect combination of love and loss woven together. The love from my soon-to-be husband would support me through the loss of the mother I loved. I married Duane Peter Ruggles on July 31, 1977 one week after my 18th birthday. Duane was the first man I truly loved other than my adoptive father—and I needed him. I got pregnant with our first child right away, and in April, 1978, our son Adam was born, just 8 months before the death of my mother. I appreciated that my mother was able to plan and attend my wedding and welcome the arrival of her first grandchild before she died. My mother battled breast cancer for about 4 years and then lost the battle on December 10, 1978.

I was 19 when my mother died at a time in my life when I needed her the most. I was just married with a new baby and had no idea how to take care of an infant, be a wife and grieve the loss of my mother all at the same time. I was the oldest child with an adopted brother who was 7 years younger than me and 12 at the time of our mother's death. At 19 and a wife and new mother, I now had to step into the role of substitute mother for my 12-year-old brother. Not only did I take on the responsibility of my brother, but I was also helping my grieving father raise a son without a mother. There was no time for me to grieve because I had to be strong for the others. I would cry silently to myself in isolation when I wouldn't be caught crying, and then I would have to shift to being the strong, responsible adult. I was wearing two masks, but underneath, my pain and grief was still there unresolved and alive within every cell of my mind, body and spirit.

As life went on, as it always does, I got pregnant with our second child, and 15 months after the birth of our son, we had our daughter, Rhonda, in July of 1979. My daughter was born the day after my birthday, so it was so exciting to have my baby girl for my 20th birthday. Life seemed to be getting better as I loved being a mom and wife. I had two beautiful children and a husband I loved. I thought life was grand. We bought our first house right before the birth of our daughter, and I was making our new house a home for our family. I always wanted a family of my own. Being adopted and never feeling like I fit, it was so wonderful that I now had a real blood family—my two children who looked like me. For me, my children healed my wounds of being adopted.

On November 11, 1980, my life would be forever changed again. On that cold autumn evening, I got a phone call in the middle of the night from my brother-in-law, Gary telling me my husband Duane had been killed in a car accident. How could this happen? Duane was 25 and just advancing in his career as a machinist. We had a beautiful home and two beautiful children. Suddenly, I became a widow at 21 with 2 toddlers. The man who had supported me from the time I was 15 through my mother's battle with cancer and her death was now gone from my life in one evening. I was alone, scared and I didn't have a clue what to do. There's no protocol for becoming a widow at 21 with two children. The two closest people to me in the world were gone—and I was devastated. How do I go on?

Life goes on and those who supported me through those first few weeks after Duane's death had now gone back to their own lives. But my life was torn apart and shattered forever. Everything I'd ever dreamed about and lived for was now gone. Yet it was clear to me that I had to go on for my children, even though I wished I could die too. It was my children who motivated me to get out of bed every morning and continue with life. However, I started drinking wine and taking prescription drugs almost daily to fill the void in my heart. I knew I had created a problem, but I needed to get through the day, to sleep at night and to try not feel anything. I was just going through the motions of life and numbing my feelings, because I knew if I gave into my emotions, I would surely fall completely apart. The trauma, the shock, the loss, the grief—these were in every cell of my mind, body and spirit. I didn't know what to do or how to fix the incessant pain and heartbreak. You might understand what it feels like if you too ever lost someone you loved so much that there's nothing to help the emotional pain and heartbreak.

After a year of numbing the pain, crying and soul searching, a good friend told me something that shifted me, my consciousness and my life. He said, "Sandra, you have the ability to start a completely new life and fill it with whatever you choose, so go for it!" Within a few days of his comment, I visited a local park where Duane and I had spent some time. I began walking around the park, first very slowly, then picking up speed and power walking; then I began to run on a narrow pathway within the park. While my body was in that place of releasing my stress and grief, I heard a voice. God's voice told me I should move to California to start a new life and that I should have faith and go. At that moment, I began to look at life differently, and I decided to travel to find myself and a new dream. I took my two children to Florida and then to California to visit and find my new beginning.

I decided to relocate with my two children to Sacramento, California from Rochester, New York to go back to school and get a college degree. I had two cousins living in California, and one was like my sister while growing up in Rochester, so I was looking forward to living close to her again. It was very hard for me to stay in Rochester in the home I had with Duane, because I was haunted by memories of the past. It was a constant reminder of what I no longer had in my life, and I definitely needed a new environment to fully embrace my new future. I found that I loved California and decided to stay and make it my new home. So, I rented out my home in Rochester and left for California taking only the things that I needed to start a new life. It was a new beginning for me and my children. It was time to move forward towards the future and leave behind the painful past I'd endured.

Life got better in California for me. Eventually, I sold the home I had bought with my husband Duane and bought a new home in Sacramento just in time for my kids to attend school. I spent the next 9 years working towards my college degree while working in Real Estate and raising my children. I had two long-term relationships during that 9 years, but I wasn't interested in marriage or having more children. Being a single mom, a college student and working was all I could handle as I created a new life.

However, after graduating from California State University Sacramento with a B.S. Degree in Business Administration, I met a man and decided to get married again in 1992. I thought my Prince Charming had arrived. He was a well-established, wealthy real estate developer with the lifestyle of the rich and famous. After years of being a single mom, college student and working hard to be sole supporter for my family, I was in love and well taken care of. We had a beautiful hilltop custom home in Napa, California, a yacht to sail the San Francisco Bay and a lifestyle of luxury with maids, gardeners and attendants. After 3 years of marriage, I knew I had made a big mistake and we divorced in 1995. It was an unhealthy marriage and the divorce dragged on for a year and a half. I left the marriage with only my personal belongings and went back to live in my home in Sacramento. Once again, I was starting over after the loss of my marriage and what I thought my life was to be. Now what? This time, though, it was clear to me that I was dealing with cumulative grief and loss, and it was in every cell of my mind, body and spirit.

After returning to Sacramento to live in my own home with my children, I reunited with friends and started dating again. It was at this time that

I started dating a good friend. We dated for a year and lived together for four years and then in the year 2000 we got married. This is the marriage that has currently ended as I write this book. During this 17 year relationship and 12 year marriage, my children left home, got married and had children of their own. I went through the empty nest syndrome when my children left home. It was not an easy time for me when they left after being a single mom for all those years and then to finally be alone without my children. It was at this time that I really realized what my husband and I had together and realized that we had grown miles apart. I had created a life without him as my children created their lives because he wasn't interested in those things that I had grown to love. We loved each other but had two separate lives. It was during my separation from him and my search for self-discovery that I found myself and the self-love that had been missing all those years. What I wanted in my life and what was in front of me were miles apart, and I had to make some changes. So I did! This has resulted in the writing of this book, Unlocking The Grief Code, and the "soul"utions for healing the mind, body and spirit.

However, the past 5 years had really become the catalyst for my healing and helping others heal from their grief and loss. My Dad got ill and was diagnosed with dementia in 2007. In 2009, he was hospitalized for about a month after an accidental fall and the thought of losing him threw me into a tailspin. At the same time my Dad was hospitalized, I had been laid off from my current position where I had worked as an Asset Manager for a well known established bank that had just gone through a long and drawn out bank takeover. This was a very stressful time in my life. Everything in my life was changing and shifting. Also during this time, my adult children couldn't handle my emotional state and they refused to see or talk to me. They refused to let me see my 4 grandchildren as well. I was devastated by the loss, and all that cumulative grief came flushing back. The estrangement continued for years, and I had to do something about the emotional pain that I was experiencing as a result of the grief and loss.

In 2010, it became clear that my life was a unique laboratory for my life purpose of helping others heal from the emotional pain of loss and grief. My personal journey of loss over the last 50+ years had given me a Ph.D. in Grief and Loss, and I was ready to do something about it. Because of my faith and spiritual beliefs, I trusted that this was all happening for a greater purpose even if I didn't understand it. However, I couldn't live with the emotional pain anymore. You know that kind of pain that just takes you out of the game of life and holds you hostage in every aspect of life. I was stuck and couldn't move forward; I couldn't go back and I didn't know what to do to relieve the emotional pain I was feeling. I had no control over what was happening, and I had come to terms with surrendering to my higher power, accepting my situation and forgiving myself and everyone involved. That's when I began to feel better, and the emotional pain I had endured was finally going away.

I knew that I was experiencing what is known as "The Dark Night of the Soul". This is when you can't go back to the life you had, you're stuck in the pain and loss of the present and the only way through the pain and loss is to feel it, heal it and move forward. *Move forward to what?* That's the million dollar question.

My identity was changing to someone I didn't quite know yet. The roles we play in life are suddenly interrupted by death, divorce, family estrangements, job loss or any type of transition where we don't know who we are anymore, where we're going next, where we fit and what to do about it. While dealing with the emotional pain and loss, we're forced to look at every aspect of our life. This is where I was, and maybe you're there right now too. This book is for you to use as a guide with tools to heal your emotional pain more quickly and easily than I was able to. According to *Time Magazine* statistics, it takes 5 to 10 years to heal from grief due to a loss. With the right coach, support and tools for grief recovery, I can promise you it doesn't have to take that long!

Chapter 2

No More Victim Consciousness

The Serenity Prayer

*GOD grant me the serenity to accept the things I cannot change
The courage to change the things I can
And the wisdom to know the difference*

ARE YOU FEELING VICTIMIZED DUE to your loss? Do you feel that the loss you've experienced is keeping you stuck? Are you resisting the change? It shouldn't have happened, or you may blame others for your grief and loss. It's easy to fall into the mindset of being a victim after experiencing grief and loss in your life. I played that role for many years. I felt broken and that somehow God had abandoned me. After my husband Duane died, I had asked a priest to help me understand why an all-loving God would take my husband and the father of my children away at the young age of 25. His answers to my questions did not help me release the grief of the pain and loss inside my heart. I still felt like a victim, and I used that mindset to feel sorry for myself and my children for years. After all, if you'd had all the loss I experienced, you would feel like a victim of circumstances too, right? Wrong! As

I held on to the belief system of victim consciousness, I continued to play the role of the victim and continued to attract more struggles and challenges into my life.

What we put out to the world is exactly what we get back. The Bible tells us, "What we sow, so shall we reap" and this is one of the Universal laws of Cause and Effect. Every effect has a cause and you must ask yourself, "What did I create or cause to produce this effect?" This one question alone will allow your mind to shift your thinking from victim to empowered. You have the ability to choose your thoughts and your actions related to those thoughts to produce a different effect or result.

How does this relate to the death of a loved one when that seems to be beyond your control, right? When those external circumstances show up that appear to be beyond your control, you always have a choice to look at life through the eyes of the victim or through the eyes of the empowered one. We all must leave this physical existence at some point. Let's face that Universal Truth. Some of us will be here longer than others. I believe we choose our time to leave this human existence and transition to another existence. We're eternal beings, so we never die—we just transform our energy and spirit to a different form and a new existence.

When we look at death or loss as a natural occurrence, and we see that grief is a normal and natural reaction to loss of any kind, then we see that the feelings and emotions are normal and natural for us. You're not abnormal for having these feelings, in fact, you're quite normal. It's only that our society hasn't taught us how to deal with loss and grief in a healthy way. By choosing an empowered approach, you'll heal faster and easier than by taking on the victim consciousness. In this book, you'll find many roadmaps to help you implement an empowered mindset to ease your pain and help you heal in a simple, speedy way.

Can you imagine for a minute that Jesus was a victim? I would like you to imagine Jesus blaming all his disciples for turning their back on him and denying they even knew him. Imagine Jesus saying, "It's all their fault that I'm being crucified on the cross." Just imagine him talking about his disciples and followers as traders, rebels and those who can't be trusted. Just imagine Jesus saying, "What's going to happen to me now that everyone has turned their backs on me?" This would be a very different effect or outcome than if he said, "Father, please forgive them for they do not know what they have done." A lot can be learned here about **acceptance, forgiveness** and **surrender**. For these are the three most important ingredients in healing grief and loss.

THE POWER OF ACCEPTANCE

The power of acceptance is the first tool that will help you heal the emotional pain from grief and loss. When you can accept what has happened as if it was meant to be, it's for your highest good or that you've chosen it, you've shifted yourself from the victim consciousness to taking full responsibility for your life in the present. God makes no mistakes, and everything that happens is happening for our highest good, even though at the time it doesn't seem that way. The power of acceptance will shift your mindset to a place where you'll see the world empowered. You'll make new choices for yourself and not live in the past. When you dwell in the past or the future, you're not living in the present moment where you have control over your life.

You may have heard the phrase, "What you resist persists". When you resist what's happening in your life, you create stress for yourself. Stress can create illness in the body and is very disempowering. Acceptance of a death, divorce, family estrangement, job loss or any type of loss frees your energy to move forward in life and to focus on the actions necessary for you to be positive, happy and at peace. You're then back in the flow of life and can start the process of deciding what's next and how you can best live in the world.

I've included a prayer for the Power of Acceptance that was written for my book by a good friend of mine, Connie Vaughn. Connie's gift from God is writing Affirmative Prayers for different situations in life. I asked

Connie to write a prayer for the Power of Acceptance so everyone who reads my book can benefit and enjoy the healing energy of this prayer. It's helpful to say this prayer when you're struggling with accepting anything in your life. You can read the prayer in the morning when you get up and again in the evening before you go to bed to help you with acceptance in your life.

Affirmative Prayer for the Power of Acceptance

In the infinity of life where I exist, all is perfect, whole and complete. I am connected to this perfection, the One Consciousness, on such a profound level as to know no separation. To see with the One Eye, Think with the One Mind and Know with the One Divine Right Order.

I know that accepting every person, place and thing exactly as it is now is perfect, whole and complete. Knowing that the Divine is pressing the good against me, I accept situations exactly as they are easily and without effort. Life is a plan, a path with which I walk. As I walk this path accepting the all good, knowing the all good and receiving the all good, my life begins to out-picture a beautiful truth. I am blessed and grateful for this knowing, this acceptance of the Divine Right Order. Living life as it unfolds, I open up to and reawaken to the infinite possibilities. I know that each situation unfolds to yet another perfect sequence of Divine Unfolding. I am the Divine seeking the Divine, and there is a deep and core acceptance within me. I bask in my life as perfectly ordered and know that great things are coming onto my path now. I reach down and pick up glorious nuggets of truth and wisdom on this path, easily accepting each nugget as a gift of the Divine.

I release anything unlike this acceptance and allow it to float to the native nothingness from whence it came. Knowing acceptance as the key that unlocks the door to my happiness and joy, I turn the lock and flow gracefully into the acceptance of the Divine Right Order. So easy, so comfortable, so relaxing...easily and effortlessly.

Thank you God for this gift of acceptance. I open it now and begin using it right away.

And so it is.

By Connie Vaughn

THE POWER OF SURRENDER

In times of deep emotional pain due to grief and loss, the best way to get through it is to surrender it to a higher power, God or Spirit. For me, the internal emotions and the pain were too much, and the only way I could deal with it was to surrender. I had to admit that I had no control over other people and external circumstances and all I could do was go with the flow, meditate, pray and wait to get the answers from God on where I would go next.

Once you have complete acceptance of the loss, you can then surrender it. In surrender, you have faith and trust that something bigger than what you can imagine is unfolding in your life and you have no control over it. In the case of my husband's death which was very sudden, my world changed overnight and there were no answers or solutions as to how I would move forward. When I surrendered the loss to God and the Universe, I was guided in ways I never could have imagined to a new life that was unfolding perfectly in the Divine plan of leading me to the next chapter in my life.

You may think that surrender is passive, but it's actually an active process. You give your grief and loss over to a higher power, you pay attention to where life is leading you next and then you follow the guidance day by day. It takes tremendous trust, faith and courage to live your life this way, but sometimes when you're stuck in the emotional pain of grief and loss, it's all you can do just to get out of bed and make it through the day. The only way is to surrender it and wait for the guidance. Unfortunately, it can't be rushed. In the flows and cycles of life, there's a time and season for everything that's divinely guided beyond your control and it's your personal responsibility to listen for the guidance and then take the necessary action steps to move forward when you are guided to do so.

This also includes surrendering people, places and circumstances beyond your control. There are those things you have no control over in your life that you must surrender to God. When I became estranged from my children and there was no communication, I tried everything possible to reconnect with them. I sent letters of apology, emails and phone calls for 3 years. This was something I clearly had no control over nor did I understand it. I didn't understand how the children I loved with all my heart and soul, that I raised as a single parent for all those years could reject me in such an abrupt way. The only way to deal with this was to surrender it to God, know that this was God's will for us at this time and that the plan was unfolding exactly the way it was supposed to happen. When my husband and mother died, it was the same scenario; it was too big for me to handle and a greater plan was unfolding that I didn't understand. All I could do was have complete acceptance of it and then surrender it.

There are actually 3 things that happen during a surrendering process. First, there will be a strong feeling of release and of letting go. Then you will experience a feeling of great relief as a result. You won't want it to be over, because this experience feels so comfortable. Sometimes surrendering is the best course of action when experiencing circumstances that are so out of control and you are in the eye of the storm.

On a final note, this book is a direct result of my surrender. For years, I'd heard the words from the Divine Intelligence to write this book but didn't pay attention because I wasn't ready to write it yet. I decided to surrender and write the book—it's clearly an example of letting go and letting God direct me. I know that in my surrender, what appeared to me is my life purpose. My life struggles, emotional pain, grief and loss were all leading up to writing this book to help all of you reading it today. You may not know what your Divine plan is, but you must accept then surrender to find out. As you take that next step forward, more is revealed; then you take another step and another step, and before you know it, you're on your pathway to the peaceful heart. Releasing the old makes way for the new in your life. It's in the Divine plan for all of us, so allow yourself to accept, surrender and see what unfolds in your life.

Affirmative Prayer for the Power of Surrender

Letting go and letting God in my life is moving to the winning side. When once surrender meant losing something, it now means moving easily and effortlessly into the flow of the Divine Right Order. Moving to the winning side, I readily find myself surrendering to God's Divine Grace. I am immersed in Grace. I feel the embrace of Grace wrapped around me like a warm, comforting blanket. So soft, so sweet is this that I readily and easily accept its power as my own.

I am one with this Infinite power and I claim it now. I know my own truth. I am a powerful, Divine being of light, love and wisdom. Coming into my own truth, my own power, I can let go and allow life to unfold in delicious waves of infinite possibilities. My life is good. My life is so very, very good right now. I feel it; I claim it; I live it.

And so it is.

By Connie Vaughn

The Healing Power Of Forgiveness

"Forgiveness is…..the means for correcting our misperceptions."

—*Gerald Jampolsky*

THE HEALING POWER OF FORGIVENESS is so important that it warrants an entire chapter of its own. Forgiveness is a powerful force for healing the mind, body and the spirit from the emotional pain due to grief and loss.

One of the most frequent comments made by those in grief is that they blame themselves that somehow they were responsible for the loss. Also, they may blame others for what has happened. I'm here to tell you that you must forgive yourself first as you release the past, and then forgive others as you did yourself.

Forgiveness doesn't mean that what happened or what you did to another was alright. It just means you're no longer willing to carry the resentment, fear or anger that accompanies blame, which turns emotions into toxic poison and hurts your spirit, your mind and your biology. It's as if you were drinking the poison and expecting someone else to die. Instead, lack of forgiveness blocks and clogs the higher energies of joy, happiness, peace and love from moving within and through you. You only have so much energy available to you on a daily basis, and it's how you use this energy that will result in your ultimate happiness and healing. If you're having thoughts of anger, resentment, blame, guilt, shame, fear or any of these that keep you "stuck" in your emotional pain, then shifting to forgiveness of yourself and others will lead you on the pathway of the peaceful heart.

The Course in Miracles is a book written and based on Christian statements and Universal Spiritual Principles. This book was written in the 1930s by two people, Helen Schucman and William Thetford, Professors of Medical Psychology at Columbia University's College of Physicians and Surgeons in New York City. The book was channeled through Helen and then became known as The Course In Miracles. It's divided into three different parts: a 669-page Text, a 488-page Workbook for students and a 92-page Manual for Teachers. This set of books is studied throughout the world today.

The Course in Miracles speaks a lot about forgiveness and includes many lessons on forgiveness. This is a great book to learn how to heal through forgiveness of yourself and others when the lessons are studied and put into daily practice. Here is my favorite section about forgiveness from the Workbook for Students that I would love to share.

Lesson 122 – Forgiveness offers everything I want.

1. What could you want that forgiveness cannot give? Do you want

peace? Forgiveness offers it. Do you want happiness, a quiet mind, a certainty of purpose and a sense of worth and beauty that transcends the world? Do you want care and safety, and the warmth of sure protection always? Do you want a quietness that cannot be disturbed, a gentleness that never can be hurt, a deep abiding comfort and a rest so perfect it can never be upset?

2. All this forgiveness offers you, and more. It sparkles on your eyes as you awake, and gives you joy with which to meet the day. It soothes your forehead while you sleep, and rests upon your eyelids so you see no dreams of fear and evil, malice and attack. And when you awake again, it offers you another day of happiness and peace. All this forgiveness offers you and more.

The Course in Miracles, Workbook, page 217.

What I would like to add about forgiveness is that it must come from the heart and soul. You must love yourself and others unconditionally if you're to truly heal from the emotional pain of grief. Your perception is your projection out to the world. You can only see your outer world based on your internal world. It is never the other way around. Therefore, your perspective about the wrong committed is only your perception and may not even be the real truth. So, to forgive is to give and receive the blessings of freedom, love, peace, joy and compassion for yourself. What you give out to the world is exactly what's given back to you. So forgive freely as you would like to have done onto you.

The Forgiveness Process For Healing

There are many different forgiveness processes for healing, but I would like to introduce to you the one I like to use for myself and my coaching clients.

This process will take about 20 to 30 minutes from beginning to end. You can do this at any time you feel you would benefit by this short process to release the old and cut the energetic ties. Ultimately, all forgiveness is for you.

1. Sit comfortably on the floor or upright in a chair.

2. Close your eyes.

3. Take 3 deep breaths, in and out…in and out…in and out.

4. Picture yourself rising up to the heavens and watching below you.

5. There below you is a gathering spot for your family and friends.

6. Begin inviting everyone you know to this gathering spot. Those who you would like to forgive in your life. You can forgive and release those who are no longer alive as well.

7. When you have mentally envisioned everyone in your past and current life in the gathering spot, you can ask them to remain in the gathering spot or leave the gathering spot. You offer forgiveness to all the stage at that time.

8. For those you want to release, see a sharp knife or sword coming down and chopping your energetic connection to these people, places or things. Let them go for the highest good for all.

9. You may decide to let go of some of them permanently or let them go so you can reconnect in a healthier manner with forgiveness. You can decide.

10. Now breathe in and out several times slowly and deeply.

11. Open your eyes and feel a sense of peace, happiness and unconditional love.

You'll find this process helpful on your path to forgiveness. Don't be surprised if you get a phone call, an email or some type of communication from someone within your circle when this process is performed. Everything is energy, so all is felt on the subtle, energetic levels as well. Your friends or family members may be sensing the shift in forgiveness and release and may want to reconnect on a much healthier level. You have the ability to decide for yourself if this is something you want. Try this process when you're experiencing the emotional pain of grief, and you'll see a real shift in your perception and thoughts when complete forgiveness is felt in the heart and soul. Unconditional love of yourself and others is the key to forgiveness.

Another treatment for healing yourself is the Affirmative Prayer for the Power of Forgiveness. This is a spiritual prayer which declares that you already have forgiven and you're a complete holistic being unified with God and the Universe. When you can see that the act of forgiveness is already done, then it's declared as such and there's a release of the outcome to the Universe—a complete release and letting go will take place. It's in the hands of the Divine Intelligence and all is perfect in the eyes of God. And so it is!

Affirmative Prayer for The Power of Forgiveness

Complete and utter forgiveness is the closest thing we have on this earth walk to unconditional love. Forgiveness does not mean we are saying what you did was okay. Forgiveness is saying I love myself too much not to forgive. I am loving myself unconditionally by forgiving others. I love me. I absolutely love me with such sweet abandon as to be surprised by how uplifted and light I feel when I practice forgiveness.

Forgiveness says I love myself so much that I no longer carry this burden of resentment. God has already forgiven, therefore God as me forgives easily as well. Being in my own power, I know that the good is restored. Perfect balance and harmony are my life now. I feel such sweet love for all things and people, it is a joy to do everything. I find joy in my work, I find joy in my drive, I find joy in cleaning and I find joy in gardening, a good book, relaxing with friends and a good meal. Never to speak of again are these old resentments that kept me locked up. I release them now. The angels are here to carry away the last remnants of my unforgiveness, and I see it floating away on the wings of angels. I see those old resentments floating away like a balloon on the wind. You are no longer part of my consciousness, and I love myself fully and with a depth and kindness that spills forth and affects all I am. Light as a feather, I walk with bounce and joy. This is my truth and I accept it now. I release anything unlike this truth to the angels and guides as they carry it away easily and effortlessly. Thank you God for this Oneness with all things. I feel it now, and I know the Cosmic Consciousness says yes to my recovery.

And so it is.

By Connie Vaughn

Ho'oponopono for Grief and Loss

A discussion on forgiveness would not be complete without mentioning this ancient Hawaiian practice of reconciliation and forgiveness.

This is a tool that can be used to help clear the emotional and mental blocks by a deep cleansing of your soul of all errors, judgments and effects of past actions or memories that may cause grief in your life or the lives of others—including Mother Nature.

This ancient Hawaiian healing technique for forgiveness is also used in the South Pacific and Polynesian cultures of Samoa, Tahiti and New Zealand. It has been used for resolving family problems, healing from illnesses and grief and loss recovery.

These words are recited over and over again as a prayer to the Divine and the Universe.

"I AM SORRY. PLEASE FORGIVE ME.
I LOVE YOU AND I THANK YOU."

We are all at one with the Universe and God. When these words are spoken with heart and soul, this is felt in all vibrations throughout you which extend to those around you physically and those not around you physically but who can feel the energetic connection. You are energy, everything is energy and what you think, see and speak radiates out through the ethers to those you love and forgive.

You may want to write these words down where you will see them daily. Whenever you feel the need to forgive yourself or someone else you'll have the words for healing right at your fingertips.

My coaching clients and I have used this ancient Hawaiian healing technique with incredible results. I have found major shifts in relationships and what I'm attracting into my life based on this forgiveness process. You can also add the extra step by repeating the words and then cutting the "aka" cords. The "aka" cords are what the ancient Healers and Shamans believe to be connecting all living things through these energetic threads or cords which keep you energetically connected to those people, places and situations in your life. By cutting these energetic cords during the forgiveness process, you're releasing the people, places or situations to the Universe for the highest good of all concerned. You can decide if you want to cut the energetic cords permanently. Then the past can be released resulting in a new connection between the person, place or situation. Therefore, reemerging in a healthier way for the future.

To conclude this chapter on forgiveness in healing the emotional pain of grief and loss, I would like to end with another passage from *The Course In Miracles* Workbook for Students, page 401, "What is Forgiveness?"

> *Forgiveness recognizes what you thought your brother did to you has not occurred. It does not pardon sins and make them real. It sees there was no sin. And in that view are all your sins forgiven. What is sin, except a false idea about God's Son? Forgiveness merely sees its falsity, and therefore lets it go. What then is free to take its place is now the Will of God.*

This is a different perception of forgiveness than you may or may not have thought about. However, I've found it to be very helpful in my healing and in the healing of my clients experiencing the emotional pain of grief and loss. Use a couple of these processes in your daily life to be open and receptive to giving and receiving forgiveness. This will shift your life to a much happier existence. You'll find the peace of heart, joy, passion and love once again so you can move forward in a positive direction.

The Shift Of Consciousness

"It is impossible for you to receive that which your mind refuses to accept. If you desire to receive more you need to consciously develop the ability to mentally encompass it."

—Ernest Holmes

Your Inner World

I WANT YOU TO KNOW YOU'RE in the right place, right here, right now to learn more about how to shift your consciousness when you're experiencing the emotional pain of grief and loss. Why is this so important? All change that occurs in life is about personally growing and evolving the soul to a higher consciousness. Albert Einstein said, "You cannot solve a problem with the same level of thinking that created the problem." Therefore, a shift in consciousness must take place to change the emotional pain you may experience in grief and loss.

What is consciousness? That's a complex question to answer and there are volumes of books written on this topic. However, for the purpose of this book to help you heal from the pain of grief and loss, consciousness can be explained as a state of awareness that results from our experiences in the external physical, mental and emotional worlds. It's known as "ordinary consciousness" and can be explained as it relates to the 5 senses—what we see, hear, touch, taste and smell in our reality. Another level of consciousness, known as "non-ordinary consciousness" can occur from that which we can't see, hear, touch, taste or smell. This shows up in life as imagination, creativity, dreams, intuition and those gut feelings we get that change our perspective. Shifting to a non-ordinary consciousness is where the healing from grief can begin to take place. When you can look beyond the world of the physical limitations of the 5 senses, you can move into a state of possibilities leading to joy, love, trust, faith and peace.

Once you shift from the physical self to the higher self, you connect with the Divine Intelligence and merge with the Oneness of the Universe and all living things. Change helps you learn, grow and move into a better place than before. Even if you can't see the blessings in the chaos of change, you must trust and have faith that you're being divinely guided towards your next destination and that this change is for your highest good.

In this chapter, I explain about the Stages of Consciousness and how to shift your consciousness to release your grief and end your painful struggles in order to move forward towards a new beginning, a new life and a new dream. This is the guiding light to happiness and peace of mind. The emotional pain comes directly from the victim consciousness and will keep you stuck in a vicious cycle of negativity and pain. This victim consciousness has such a low vibrational frequency in the mind, body and spirit that it doesn't allow the soul to evolve and grow, and it can even create illness in the body. It keeps us stuck in the old attitudes, emotions and belief systems. It keeps us stuck in life and unable to move forward to be, do and have what we want in life. It's not empowering to be a victim. In fact, it's disempowering.

Let's look at the questions that are asked by those who are in a state of grief. You'll notice the questions you're asking now as you're with your pain and loss, and this will help you move through to the next stage of evolution so you can release the grief and welcome relief.

Most likely you're in this first stage of "change" in your grief. This is the **Transition** stage. You're in a place of change and restructuring your life from the familiar to the unfamiliar. You may have lost a loved one, gone through a divorce, lost your job or found out that you have a serious health issue. In any of these cases, you're in transition. You're asking the questions: "What has happened?", "Why did this happen?", "How could this have happened", "What do I have to learn from this?", "What's next?" This is the stage where you now realize you're either "stuck" or you don't know what to do. This is when you can easily get caught up in the vicious cycle of pain that keeps you at the victim level. This is typically when you experience the "Dark Night of the Soul" because you can't stay where you are because the familiar has changed, yet you don't know where you're going next. You may have lost your belief in the connection to God and the Oneness of the Universe; you feel separate from others. Also, you may have an identity crisis at this time if you were once a wife and now your husband is gone, you were a mom and now your children are gone or you were a daughter or son and now your parent is gone. Or you had good health and now you have a health crisis or you had a career that was part of your identity and now that's gone.

At this next stage, you will experience **Awakening,** if you decide you are ready to move through the "Dark Night of the Soul" to a new beginning. You will only experience this next stage if you are ready to ask the questions of life to move you into remembering who you truly are as a spiritual being having a human experience. When someone has experienced the emotional pain of grief and loss, this is where you will decide that you can no longer live with the emotional pain and the feeling of being "stuck". You begin to awaken to your higher self through your intuition and new ideas of inspiration and imagination that begin to appear in your reality. You can no longer deny that you must take action to move forward towards the future. You may experience the

Awakening stage just by reading this book because you will begin to gather new thoughts and ideas to incorporate into your life that will catapult you forward to the next stage of self-remembring who you really are and take the necessary steps to become your true essence and evolve your soul.

At the next stage, you may ask the questions: "Who am I?", "What's my purpose?" "What's my role now?" "Why am I here?" After experiencing a loss, you realize that your life will never be the same again, but "What is next?" You start asking these important questions. This stage is about **Self-remembering** who you are in your soul essence. You must know who you are to fully embrace where you're going. At this point, you remember that you're a spiritual being having a human experience and that nothing really dies as a spiritual being. You know that energy doesn't die; it merely transforms into another existence according to quantum physics. It's important to realize that this is your internal world not the external world. You don't look outside yourself for answers; you must look within to your soul and ask for guidance from your higher self. If you're struggling with this stage, I'll be giving you some tools in my next section on healing through mind, body and spirit that will help you.

In the next stage you may find yourself becoming more into greater **Awareness** asking: "Is this all there is to life?" You may find that you're sick and tired from the pain, loss and grief and you realize you can no longer live with it anymore—something needs to change. It's at that time when you make a conscious decision to change—and you're ready for the change.

Your awareness is heightened; you're now aware that you must take the next step in your growth process. When I decided to move to California after the death of my husband and go back to college to get my education, I made the necessary environmental changes to align with the internal changes I wanted to make. For me, I needed to relocate to something new and different and leave behind the painful memories of the loss of my familiar life. This allowed me to feel better, release unwanted obstacles and create a new me. This new awareness will shift you to new beginnings and you'll begin to attract into your life all those things you desire and focus upon. What you focus on expands, and in this case your awareness does too. You'll evolve into a beautiful butterfly so you can spread your wings and fly once again. Then it's transformation time.

The next stage you encounter in your growth is **Transformation**. This stage takes courage and strength to actually move through and change those old emotions, attitudes and beliefs that are keeping you stuck in the emotional pain of grief and loss. This is the stage where you'll work with your emotions to release the unhealthy ones and replace them with positive ones. Emotions, attitudes and belief systems are not only found in your mind through thoughts, but I believe these are attached to every cell of your body. When you go through grief and loss, you experience an event that affects the cellular memory which must be addressed in the healing process. We are holistic beings and what affects our mind affects our physical body and our spirit simultaneously. Therefore, you must heal the emotions, attitudes and beliefs first to release them from the body so the spirit can be free once again. This book focuses on the stage of Transformation, where you Unlock the Grief Code in your mind, body and spirit. You'll find exercises in chapters 5 through 7 that will take you on your journey of transformation of mind, body and spirit to assist in your healing from grief and loss.

The last and final stage is known as **Transmutation**. This is the stage that allows you to manifest your heart's desire in the physical world. This is the place where miracles happen, where grief and loss no longer exist. Instead there's bliss, joy, love, happiness and peace. You're now vibrating your entire being at such a high level that even your physical body will change to accommodate the new vibrational frequencies of your higher consciousness. This is where someone with a terminal illness is suddenly cured. This is where you manifest and attract all those things you desire in life. You can't reach this place if you don't transform the emotions, attitudes and beliefs that keep you stuck in the pain of grief and loss.

These are the important stages you may encounter when evolving from the pain of grief and loss to a life of happiness, joy, love, bliss and peace. Well, I want you to know that I'm here to help you with this process—you're not alone. Please, don't do this alone. You need a support system. You need someone who understands what you're going through, who'll support you through the challenges of rebuilding your life again and can share the wisdom of grief recovery. You can heal the pain now and forever by going to my website at www.SandraRuggles.com and signing up for one of my coaching programs or healing retreats and by joining my community.

The Energy World –
The Shift in Consciousness and the Chakras

How does this shift in consciousness occur within your mind, body and spirit? One of the ways this happens is through the Chakra Energy System. According to the ancient Sanskrit writings, there are 7 chakras in the body that are known as "wheels of light" and have a bell shaped design that synthesize and communicate information from your external environment to your consciousness. There are 7 major chakras associated with the physical body. Each chakra tells a story about you, your soul and your consciousness. Therefore, when experiencing pain due to grief and loss in your external world, this information is directly communicated through the chakra energy system resulting in an energy imbalance within the 7 chakras. Each chakra must be addressed to align these energy centers in perfect harmony to return you to balance and wholeness once again.

The 7 chakras are the sacred circuitry where the mind, body and spirit meet with the Divine Source energy and merge into Oneness. These vortexes of energy are the life force centers that sustain and nourish the physical, emotional, mental and spiritual bodies. When the chakras are in balance, you'll return to a state of wholeness releasing the pain of grief and loss.

The energy flowing from the chakras directly affects your consciousness in the way you perceive and live your life after a loss. When you're in a state of any of the lower emotions such as grief, fear, anger, apathy, guilt or shame then you're living in the lower dimension of consciousness. This leads to separation from self-love, from others and from God. It becomes a lonely, dark place to be, and you only see yourself from a physical perspective. By balancing the 7 chakras, you can increase your level of consciousness to one of willingness, acceptance, love, joy and peace, moving to the higher dimensions of consciousness. This leads to union with mind, body and spirit and connection with the Divine Intelligence, and thus connection, wholeness and happiness. You truly come home to the self to live a life of your dreams.

The 7 Chakra Energy System

First Chakra – This Chakra is known as the "Root Chakra" and is considered the energy for survival such as personal safety and security. This Chakra is tied to the 5 physical senses and is located at the base of the spine between the anus and the genitals.

Second Chakra – This Chakra deals with all your relationships, sexuality and emotions. It's tied to your creativity and it's where you store your emotions. It's located in the lower abdomen and lumbar area and is connected to the reproductive organs, large and small intestine and sexual organs.

Third Chakra – This Chakra is known as the "Personal Power Chakra" and is considered to affect the functioning of the brain, all organs, all glands and all the body's major systems. It's located in the solar plexus which is the stomach and liver area of the body.

Fourth Chakra – This is known as the "Heart Chakra". This is the Chakra that's affected the most when in pain due to grief and loss. It's located in the center of your chest. The heart center is where forgiveness, love and compassion is regulated and worked with to heal you. This Chakra is the most important when healing grief and loss, because this is where there's an abundance of love, compassion, trust and passion when in balance. When not in balance, there's envy, doubt, fear, obsession and lower consciousness feelings and emotions. When in pain due to grief or loss, most people often shut down this Chakra consciously or unconsciously because they feel vulnerable to more pain and are reluctant to open up their heart in fear that they'll feel too much and be overwhelmed in feelings of grief. However, you must open this energy center to trust, have unconditional love, compassion, acceptance, forgiveness and surrender. To feel it and then to heal it, then returning to balance.

Fifth Chakra – This is the "Throat" Chakra and the way you express yourself, stand up for your belief systems and speak your truth. It's located in the center of the throat. This Chakra helps you to have faith, speak up for yourself, be assertive and have the ability to make choices that reflect who you are. When in pain due to grief or loss, you sometimes won't speak about it. Feelings and emotions withheld result in an imbalance in this Chakra. To heal, you must feel, talk and release the feelings.

Sixth Chakra – This Chakra is known as the "Third Eye" and is located in the center of the forehead between the eyebrows. This energy center allows you to see all dimensions of consciousness and is where the intuition meets with the intellect. This is the energy center for your higher intuitive self where all the answers to your questions are stored. When you're in pain due to grief and loss, this Chakra becomes blocked and imbalanced, cut off from a true sense of how to move forward. It's vital that you unblock this energy center to allow the merging of the soul's intuitive knowingness of truth with the mind to move forward in a new direction to heal the pain. This is where you can create your own reality and move ahead based on the truth of who you are now becoming after the pain of your grief and loss.

Seventh Chakra – This Chakra is known as the "Thousand Petal Lotus" according the Indian Sanskrit teachings and is located at the crown of your head. This is where the Divine energy enters the "Crown Chakra" and aligns with the other 6 Chakras below to balance you into wholeness and grounding. The Divine energy enters into your physical body and heals the pain of your grief or loss. This is the connection with Universal Consciousness and God where you receive your sacred union with the Divine Source. You can balance this Chakra through prayer and meditation increasing your Oneness and connection to God. This is where you'll find peace, inspiration, faith in a greater good and living in the present moment.

This concludes the description of the 7 Chakra Energy System and how each Chakra relates to your self-healing while experiencing the pain of grief and loss. After reading the descriptions of each Chakra and how it relates to your healing process, you may become aware of where you're out of alignment with your energy body. It's my hope that you'll look further into each opportunity to heal your energetic imbalances within the 7 Chakras so you may return to a state of wholeness again on your path to peace and living a life of your dreams. I would like to add here that there are many more Chakras located in the physical and energy bodies which are too numerous to mention in this book but should not be ignored when working with imbalances within the energy system of the physical body. I included the 7 Chakra Energy System here as a first step in the healing process. This is to shift the consciousness of the person suffering from the pain of grief and loss and to assist in moving forward to a renewed sense of wholeness.

I would like to include an exercise and some affirmations below for you to use during meditation and prayer to help you harmonize your Chakras into a state of balance.

MEDITATION EXERCISE AND AFFIRMATIONS FOR HEALING PAIN DUE TO GRIEF AND LOSS USING THE 7 CHAKRA ENERGY SYSTEM

MEDITATION

Begin by sitting in a quiet room with your eyes closed and your arms and legs uncrossed to allow free flowing energy from the top of your Crown Chakra to your Root Chakra down into Mother Earth with a straight alignment of your spine. Breathe deeply in through the nose and out through the mouth 3 times to allow the life force energy to permeate every inch of your mind, your body and your spirit. Then repeat these affirmations out loud to the Universe declaring these are true for you right here, right now in the present moment. Repeat daily in the morning upon awakening or before you go to bed in the evening. You may even want to create a sacred space with candles, incense and soft music to enhance your experience. You can be creative with this process; there's no right or wrong way to do it. Do it the way that's most comfortable and effective for you and your healing. Begin with the Crown Chakra (7th Chakra) bringing the Divine Source from God and the Universal Consciousness through the body one Chakra at a time, and align your entire being with this healing energy coming from the Divine Source. You can even give it a color to visualize it like a stream of purifying healing water running from the top of your head to the bottom of your feet and balancing you back to wholeness. Enjoy the process and happy healing!

Definition of Meditation: Listening to God

Definition of Prayer: Talking to God

Affirmations For Healing

CHAKRA 7 – CROWN CHAKRA: VIOLET
I AM connected to the Divine Source at all times in all ways.

CHAKRA 6 – THIRD EYE: INDIGO
I SEE the truth of all situations easily and effortlessly.

CHAKRA 5 – THROAT CHAKRA: BLUE
I SPEAK my truth with love and kindness.

CHAKRA 4 – HEART CHAKRA: GREEN
I FORGIVE and give unconditional love to myself and others.

CHAKRA 3 – PERSONAL POWER: YELLOW
I AM powerful.

CHAKRA 2 – RELATIONSHIPS: ORANGE
I AM abundant in all my relationships.

CHAKRA 1 – ROOT CHAKRA: RED
I AM safe and all my needs are met easily and effortlessly.

Chapter 5

Unlocking The Grief Code – Healing For The Mind

"We live for the body…We live for the mind… We live for the soul. Not one of these is better or holier than the other."

—Wallace D. Wattles

THE MIND IS THE PLACE where your consciousness speaks to you when you've experienced the emotional pain of grief and loss. A significant event occurs in your external world such as a death, divorce, estrangement, bankruptcy, foreclosure or any loss that completely changes your familiar life. It's immediately transcribed by the mind as a thought. The thought itself is not good or bad, it's just a thought—that is, until you attach meaning to it as an emotion, attitude or belief. When situations happen that are beyond your control like a death of a loved one, the first thought that may occur is one of either relief or disbelief. What happens next is a feeling is attached to the thought. A feeling is neutral until you attach an emotion to it. The thought and feeling are translated by the mind, and you're moved to action by the significant event to either a positive or negative emotion, attitude or belief. This is where the journey begins in the mind, and this is the place where healing the mind can begin with the right tools and techniques.

When my husband was killed in a car accident, the first thought that occurred to me was disbelief that what was happening was real. My mind shifted from what was real to disbelief, back and forth, stuck in the shock and trauma of a sudden death. In the case of my mother who had suffered so much due to her body being eaten away by cancer, her final breath came as one of relief at first and then followed by the pain of the grief and loss. So, these thoughts are only the beginning of an emotional roller coaster that can sometimes seem overwhelming and never ending until you look at how to heal the thoughts that move you through the pain and forward in your life to transform these thoughts of despair, hopelessness, anger, disbelief and pain to ones of peace, love, harmony and happiness.

You'll often hear "Time heals all wounds". Well, how long does it take to heal the pain from grief and loss? Is there a certain time period that's acceptable to forget and move on? I would say absolutely not. Most of you who've experienced such a loss would agree with me, I'm sure. Time doesn't heal all wounds from the pain of grief and loss. The loss will always be a part of your life; however, how you think about it can change, and that's what you do have control over in your daily life. Therefore, the healing can occur with changing your thoughts. You'll never change what has happened, but changing your thoughts about the loss will allow the pain and grief to shift and change as well.

You must take action to heal those thoughts as you would take action if you had a broken body part. You wouldn't just wait until the arm or leg healed in its own time; you would take action to go to the doctor and have it casted to facilitate the healing. It's also just as important to do the necessary action steps to heal yourself from grief and loss to find happiness, joy and love once again. What are those steps, you ask? Let's look at the steps that will help you to move forward in healing your pain from grief and loss.

Step 1:
Become Aware Of Your Thoughts

All that exists in our external world produces information that appears in the mind as a thought. When experiencing grief due to a loss of any magnitude, it's processed at the base of the brain known as the Reticular Activating System. This part of the brain is responsible for many functions, one of which is to sort and filter information in the mind. This is what determines the information that comes quickly into the conscious and unconscious minds. Because we can't process all external information that comes to us at the same time, some of the information is stored in the unconscious mind and some in the conscious mind. Research indicates that only 5% of this information is stored in the conscious mind and 95% is stored in the unconscious mind. That's why working with the unconscious mind is where you can really make big changes in your life.

On a conscious level, you can pay attention to your thoughts and be readily aware of what those thoughts are in order to change them. However, the unconscious thoughts are the ones you must dig deeper to uncover and transform in order to change your life and get unstuck from the past and the vicious cycle of grief-induced pain.

Once a thought has occurred after an external event, it creates a feeling. A feeling is just information about the thought and doesn't have a negative or positive result. A feeling is a normal reaction to something that's happened, and in the case of grief and loss, it can trigger an emotional reaction or state of mind. This internal state of mind quickly releases chemicals into the entire nervous system which affects your mind as well as every cell of your body; this is the mind-body connection. An energetic emotional charge is set into motion which results in making you feel angry, sad, fearful, frustrated or in pain. This is known as the "fight or flight" response that's typically set into motion after an external event occurs that threatens you in some way. On the other hand, it can also trigger the positive emotions of love, joy, courage and hope if there's an external event that occurs that is positive. Therefore, the thoughts and resulting emotions are where you can create change when experiencing the emotional pain of grief.

STEP 2:
BECOME AWARE OF YOUR EMOTIONS, ATTITUDES AND BELIEFS THAT ARE KEEPING YOU STUCK IN YOUR EMOTIONAL PAIN AND SUFFERING.

Your emotions, attitudes and beliefs in relation to your "State of Mind" hold the key to your healing. You may think you have no control over your emotions, but there's always choice to stay with any emotion such as grief. This emotion may be keeping you stuck in the vicious cycle of pain and hurting you, yet you're not even aware that this is the cause of your pain. When I was experiencing my devastating pain after my husband's death, it never occurred to me that what I was experiencing was grief due to the loss. I just knew I was in pain, and I was looking for anything to help me relieve this emotional pain. Once I was introduced to the emotion of grief, I was able to look at it as only an emotion that didn't have control over me. Standing as the observer watching the emotion of grief in my life, I was able to detach from it as a stranger and see it as just an emotion. The grief in truth wasn't me or who I was in my true essence, but something I had attached to by my thoughts and feelings. What this meant to me was that this emotion could be changed by exchanging it for a more positive one, thus making a different choice in my life. I could try on the new emotions of love and compassion for myself and see how that fit for me in the present moment. I have to say it felt much better than the pain, and from then the healing towards peace of mind happened almost immediately.

Emotion is defined as "energy in motion", and I found I could change this energy with a different state of mind. I learned I could make the decision to exchange it for happiness, so I just made the decision to be happy! Then I moved forward into action to achieve my desired result. Happiness does NOT come from the external world—it's truly an inside job.

The internal signals triggered from an external event may be made up of pictures (visual), sounds (auditory), sensations (kinesthetic), smells (olfactory) and tastes (gustatory). Everything you experience is taken in through the 5 senses. In changing your internal world through the 5 senses, you must change the pictures (your visions and dreams), the sounds (self-talk and inner dialogue), sensations (exercise and feeling), smells (healthy environment) and tastes (healthy organic foods). By making small changes in all of these senses, you can create a new life and transform the grief you're experiencing to happiness and peace.

I'm going to add another sense, a sixth sense, known as "intuition". Listening to your intuition about a situation can lead you out of your mind into your heart, shifting your state of mind to a more positive one. When you combine this intuition with your heart center, you can connect with the path of healing the pain and return to happiness. It takes great faith and trust to follow intuition, and it ultimately leads you to a place of great clarity and peace. When you pay attention to that inner knowing about a situation, you'll get guidance about the necessary action steps you need to take to move forward. Everyone has intuition although some people tell me they don't know how to tap into it or don't know if they can trust it. Accessing your intuition is like connecting with your inner compass, and it can be cultivated with practice. It's really like a muscle in your body—the more you use it the stronger it becomes. You'll be led to the answers you're seeking. Meditation is one great way to access your intuition, and journaling is another. I'll be talking more about these two channels for your intuition later in this chapter and again in chapter 7 on Healing the Spirit.

ATTITUDES

Attitudes, like emotions, have judgment and can be positive or negative. These represent groupings of beliefs and values you may have from past or current external experiences. This represents your "frame of mind" and is how you see the world. Are you seeing the world as the glass half full or glass half empty? When you're in pain as a result of grief or loss, your attitude may be the only thing keeping you from finding the happiness, joy, peace and love you're seeking. *How do you change your attitude?* Well, let's look closely at values and beliefs.

VALUES

Your values are what you consider important in life; then your behavior is guided based on these values. They determine your character and how you live your life. Values can be driven and lived out from the conscious mind as well as the unconscious mind. For example, if you say you value your family, but most of your time and energy is spent working at your job or career, then this would be a situation where your conscious mind says one thing, but your unconscious mind is driving your actual behavior. You would be out of alignment with your values.

Recognizing and aligning your conscious and unconscious values will move you toward being happy and getting what you truly desire. You would then be "walking your talk" and "living your truth". This is where the conscious and unconscious minds are aligned in perfect harmony to achieve happiness, contentment and fulfillment.

However, when experiencing the emotional pain of grief due to a loss, your conscious and unconscious values often shift and change, and you have to reevaluate and realign your values. When you value a relationship, a job or your health and then experience a loss in one of these parts of life, this can be shattering to you as your values must shift due to your external circumstances.

I use myself as an example of how this can happen. I had placed a very high value in my life of being a mother and grandmother. I love my children and grandchildren and when making decisions about how I live my life, I would always consider them in my decision-making. However, after the estrangement from my children, my conscious mind was fully aware that this value was now absent from my life. My unconscious mind still held tightly to this value, because it was a deep value ingrained in me for over 30 years. This incongruency of the conscious mind vs. the unconscious mind resulted in the emotional pain and grief due to this loss beyond my control in my external world. After working with a grief coach, I was able to clearly recognize and align my conscious and unconscious mind to reduce the pain and move forward into peace of mind, self-love, joy and happiness once again. The estrangement and the external world had not changed, but the transformation inside me had, and that made all the difference for me in my world.

BELIEFS

Your beliefs are what determine how you live your life and are created by your attitudes and emotions. Your belief system contributes to your perceptions of the world and to your life in general. Your beliefs lead to your habits and repetitive behaviors and support your "state of mind". Some of your beliefs no longer serve you, but you continue to hang on to them because it's comfortable. However, positive change can happen from releasing your limited, unproductive beliefs and expanding your consciousness beyond these boundary conditions of your current belief systems.

When experiencing emotional pain due to grief and loss, the beliefs you have may keep you from moving forward and experiencing all that life has to offer. It's helpful to look at current beliefs that keep you "stuck" in this emotional pain. For example, you may have lost a job after 30 years working in the same occupation at the same company. You're devastated by this loss because you've been there for so many years and this job has become part of your identity. You may have the belief that you won't find another job similar to the one you lost and with the same pay. Also, you may have the belief that you're too old to start over in a new field of work, so you're in a downward spiral of emotional pain and grief due to the loss. You may find yourself "stuck" unable to move forward past the beliefs keeping you in the same place. Changing these limiting beliefs is the challenge for most people, but if you realize that the belief system is the problem, then a shift can occur from one of a victim to being empowered. A new belief is put in place of the old belief, and it may support you in taking the opportunity to change jobs or careers into something you've always wanted to do all your life. It could be creating a new career out of hobby you've had and now you'll start a new business. It may be that you decide to take a year off and travel to see the world and explore what's next. There are many new belief systems that can be exchanged for the ones that are no longer serving you.

It's valuable to note that whatever belief system you have is determining what you are attracting into your life—NOW! The Law of Attraction applies here showing you that your outer world is a mirror reflection of your inner world. So, if you want to change your outer world in some way, you must begin with your inner world and your belief system.

Step 3:
Start A Daily Meditation Practice
For At Least 15 Minutes

Meditation is an important practice to integrate into your daily routine when you're experiencing the emotional pain of grief and loss. Starting a meditation practice will help you to heal faster and easier than you can imagine. Many different meditation techniques promote relaxation, increased energy, connection with God or the Divine Intelligence, enhanced intuition and much more. You'll find that with a regular meditation practice you'll have an overall sense of well-being as a result—which facilitates the healing process. Meditation is also a gateway to receiving information and guidance that will help you to heal. You'll be more able to tap into your intuition and your mind for clarity and peace. You'll also develop a positive mindset which will allow you to feel compassion, forgiveness, love, joy and peace of mind and to release anger, fear, shame, guilt and other negative emotions. Imagine transforming all those negative emotions to the beautiful positive ones that will assist with your healing "soul"utions—all with a regular meditation practice.

Thousands of research studies about meditation and its health benefits have been published. Some of these benefits include stress reduction, changes in metabolism, lowered blood pressure, pain reduction and brain activation. Meditation literally changes your biology so the body functions are flowing without resistance.

Many types of meditation are available to you, depending on various religious traditions, such as Buddhism. If there's a particular tradition you practice then you may already be familiar with a certain type of meditation. However, if you're new to the idea of meditation and haven't meditated before, I have a few suggestions to get you started.

How To Get Started with a Meditation Practice

1. Start out with short segments of around 10 to 15 minutes once a day either in the morning after you awaken or before you go to bed. You can create a practice during the middle of the day if morning or evening isn't convenient for you and your schedule.

2. Find a place in your home or office where you won't be disturbed during the time you're meditating.

3. Create a sacred space just for your meditation practice and add candles, a CD or MP3 player for meditation music, a comfortable chair or floor mat with pillows and perhaps some sacred objects like crystals or religious statues or photos.

4. Sit with a straight spine in a chair or sit in a cross- legged lotus position on the floor.

5. Close your eyes and take three deep breaths in through the nose and out through the mouth.

6. Sit with palms facing up on your lap.

7. Place the tip of your tongue on the roof of your mouth.

8. Relax your body by scanning from the bottom of your feet to the top of your head releasing any tension, stress or tightness and allowing your energy to flow freely.

9. Sit in silence while preparing your mind to go into nothingness (the void). Thoughts may come, but release them as soon as they surface in your mind. It will take time to sink deeper and deeper into the void, so be patient with yourself. You may want to use a mantra, book passage, or affirmation to repeat over and over again to focus your mind.

10. You may also listen to a guided music meditation CD, MP3 or tape.

11. Keep a journal next to you so you can write down your thoughts and insights when your meditation session is complete. You'll be amazed at what you'll learn about yourself.

12. Practice, practice and more practice!

If you find you need help getting the feel of meditating, you can find many great books and classes on meditation practices. Check my website to find my schedule of workshops, classes and retreats for meditation and more. Join my community and learn about meditation and other healing techniques.

Step 4:
Create A Vision Board Of What You Want To Create In Your Life

A Vision Board is a great visualization tool to manifest what you'd like to create in your life after experiencing a transition. Life as you've known it has changed and now you're transforming your world in a new and different way. You know things have changed or will have to change, so this is the time to determine: "to what?" To go from where you are to where you want to be requires some thought—then action.

Often during times of grief and loss, you may know what you don't want and you know the truth and the reality of what's happened, but if you could script your life from that point forward, what would it look like? You must first accept the loss and change to move forward from "what was" to "what will be". A Vision Board can help you do this.

A Vision Board can take you anywhere from 1 to 5 hours to create. That really depends on you. To create a Vision Board, you must first find some old magazines, books or newspapers. I always like to go to the bookstore or drug store and purchase new magazines that represent the things I enjoy or that I would like to incorporate into my life. You can gather old photographs, new photographs or any pictures you may have representing things you love. You're going to make a collage, so gather together all items and pictures, etc. that you want to include on your Vision Board. You'll need a big piece of cardboard or posterboard to affix all photos to with enough space for all those pictures and visions you would like to create. Any office supply store will have large pieces of cardboard—either white or colored—or you may have some around the house. Place everything on a flat surface like a kitchen or dining room table. Besides your pictures and board, you'll need scissors, glue, glue gun or tape readily available to affix your photos to the cardboard. Now you're ready to begin…..

You'll look through the magazines, books, newspapers and photographs to see what jumps out at you that you absolutely without a doubt want to include in your new life. This can be anything visual like a picture or it can be words, symbols or an actual item like coins or dollar bills. Use your imagination about what you want to bring forth into your life now. I suggest you dream big with no limitations to open up your mind to new possibilities you may not have imagined before your life-changing event. Take your time going through the visual items, and be conscious of what you want your life to consist of after your loss. Remember that you must have already come to an acceptance and surrender that the past is the past and the only way to move forward is to stay in the present moment while creating a new future for yourself. This process may bring up a lot of emotion for you, so just accept the feelings for what they are and move through them. You have to feel it to heal it. This process is all about healing your mind, body and spirit.

Once you have all your visuals glued onto the board in a collage format, you're ready to hang this beautiful new beginning pictorial somewhere you'll see it every day. You can frame it and hang it or just hang it as it— it's up to you. However, it's necessary for you to look at it daily, because you'll begin to attract those things into your life. What you focus on expands and manifests into form, so you now have these visuals in your mind, body and spirit to bring them forward into your life. Enjoy the process and have fun!

STEP 5:
CREATE A GRATITUDE JOURNAL AND WRITE DAILY ABOUT YOUR THOUGHTS, DREAMS, DESIRES AND IDEAS

A daily practice of writing in a Gratitude Journal will help you tremendously with getting more in touch with your thoughts, desires, dreams and ideas. One of the reasons I've enjoyed this daily practice is because it's allowed me to take the thoughts in my mind and get them down on paper to view them from a new perspective. There's something magical that happens when you begin to realize what you're thinking about and get it down on paper. This has been a tremendous healing tool for me when I was in the dark night of despair. When I read what I'd written, it took on an entirely new dimension, because I was able to look at this information from the observer, from outside myself and begin to notice what I needed to change to be happy. When you can look at what you've written as if someone else has written it, you begin to notice thoughts and patterns of behavior you may want to release, because they no longer serve you for your highest good. You may also notice what you love about your life and what you want to incorporate more of, that is, what makes you feel important and joyful, what makes your heart sing. When you actively participate in your own healing from grief and loss, you've found the key to unlocking the grief code in your mind.

One of the important keys to writing in your gratitude journal is that you'll learn to expand your mind as you learn to disconnect from your pain and discontentment. You'll get in touch with what you're no longer happy with in your life and replace these with your dreams and desires. You'll come to realize more of what those things are, and you'll expand your awareness of what is actually possible for you. You'll be pulled in the direction of the things you desire and want more of in your life. Use your imagination and your intuition to write in your journal and transcend the negative patterns of self-defeating behaviors that no longer serve you from your higher self. This will be empowering for you as you do this on a regular basis, and it will inspire you to go beyond what you thought you could actually do, be and have in your life. This will promote an awesome feeling within you as you feel more and more that your life is wonderful and all is well—transcending the emotional pain of grief and loss.

You'll also notice the synchronicities that happen in your life by daily gratitude journaling. Synchronicities are those events or experiences that are deemed unrelated or unlikely to occur at the same time, but they do happen simultaneously in a meaningful way that changes your life for the better. This is also referred to as "being divinely guided" by God or the Divine Intelligence in the Universe. You may also want to call these "miracles", because they can occur in miraculous ways. When you begin to notice these events as they occur and write them down in your gratitude journal giving thanks for all the blessings, then you'll see more of them happen. It's amazing when you focus on miracles, how many more you'll notice as you grow a life you love.

Rules for Manifesting Miracles

1. Write in your Gratitude Journal daily for at least 40 days to realize the greatest benefits.

2. Write at least 5 things every day that you're grateful for in your life.

3. Write everything in the positive so you begin to think and talk this way.

4. Write about the synchronicities you experience between what you write and what shows up in your life.

5. If you write something negative or self-defeating in your journal then reframe it with the positive after acknowledging it and releasing it to be healed.

6. Write in the first person present tense as though you are experiencing this now.

7. Write about what you want to create in your life and be specific.

8. Write with feeling and claim that what you desire is already yours waiting to appear in your life.

9. Stay focused on what you do want in your life and releasing what you don't want.

10. Use your imagination to write about your dreams and desires. It's not the sky's the limit, it's your mind's the limit.

11. Ask for what you want; the Universe doesn't know what to bring you unless you ASK.

Have fun with this and enjoy the process! The power of Joy also brings miracles into our lives.

Step 6:
Visualization Exercises Using The Mind As A Catalyst For Change

The process of Creative Visualization is a practice where you change your external world by changing your thoughts and expectations within the internal world. You do this by creating a detailed picture or vision of what you desire and then visualizing it over and over again anchoring it through the 5 senses.

Your power to overcome your emotional pain from grief and loss comes directly from your power within to change the mental pictures of the loss along with the negative emotions of fear, anger, shame, guilt and grief to more empowering emotions such as forgiveness, acceptance, surrender, joy, compassion, love and inner peace. You can accomplish this with creative visualization techniques and some coaching.

Studies have shown that only 10% of our happiness comes from our environment and the external world. Therefore, 90% of our happiness is derived from choices we make about things directly under our own control and from our daily habits. That means when you change those inner pictures with visualization techniques creating what you want in your life and when you have direct control over your daily habits, your happiness quotient skyrockets along with the results in your life. Professional athletes use visualization techniques in their daily trainings so they can see themselves outperforming their competition and they set goals that will make them winners of their game. You too can overcome your dark visions of pain and loss and create bright visions of what you desire and dream of.

BASIC CREATIVE VISUALIZATION PROCESS

Create a picture in your mind of what you desire to come into your life.

What do you see?

What do you feel?

What do you hear?

What do you smell?

Repeat this process daily to change the program in your mind and invite your desire to join you.

As Within, So Without

When you believe it, you will see it!

This can also be achieved through Guided Imagery where a moderator tells a story and paints a picture with words while the recipient listens. Then it's imprinted into the mind and through the 5 senses to create this in the recipient's reality. Guided imagery can be used for almost anything you'd like to transform in your life—even your health. Every thought triggers a part of the brain, your physical body and your spiritual nature. You can change the actual structure of your body, mind and spirit. By changing your visions and inner dialogue about those visions, you integrate courage, power, love, harmony and inspiration into your life and substitute these for the visions of failure, lack, limitation, fear, anger and grief. Your life will change and you'll know true joy, love, harmony, hope and peace of mind. All true happiness begins with consciousness. *Are you ready to live the life of your dreams*? You absolutely have the power to unlock the grief code within and begin your journey to wholeness!

CHAPTER 6

Unlocking The Grief Code – Healing For The Divine Physical Body

"The doctor of the future will give no medicine, but will interest his patients in the care of the human frame, in diet, and in the causes and prevention of disease."

—*Thomas Edison*

HEALING YOUR MIND IS ONE component of returning yourself to wholeness, but you must include healing the Divine body in the overall healing process. It's necessary to heal the mind, the body and the spirit to return to wholeness and complete the healing process in its entirety. When the mind, body and spirit connection are in complete balance, this results in an overall sense of well-being, inner peace, joy and happiness.

I would like to explain what happens to the physical body during the grief and loss process. The body is experiencing the trauma and change in body chemistry at the cellular level due to the effects of the mind. All illness begins in the mind and then manifests into the physical body. The mind believes the negative thoughts of distress and stress, and the resulting emotional charge is sent through the entire physical body. The emotional charge sends out signals to the body to prepare for resistance and imbalance results. When this emotional charge is experienced at the physical level for long periods of time, it creates in the physical body what we call "dis-ease". There are levels of "dis-ease" from minor to chronic to life threatening. By treating the mind, the body and the spirit together, true healing can take place permanently in your life.

Your lifestyle changes significantly when you experience grief and loss. You need to become conscious of all the ways you can support your physical body during these times of great emotional stress and distress. This includes having healthy habits and behaviors that support your mind, body and spirit to heal with the path of least resistance. Consider eating organic healthy foods, getting proper exercise, getting enough sleep, detoxifying and purifying the emotions, attitudes and beliefs, learning stress reduction techniques and getting bodywork such as massage, acupressure, acupuncture and other body therapies. These are among the most important methodologies to heal the body.

In this chapter on healing the divine body, you'll learn some of the ways to help yourself heal. Ultimately, you're in control of your own healing from the emotional pain of grief and loss. I'm sharing with you some of the ways I've learned to help heal myself as well as others I've worked with over the years. However, it's ultimately up to you to incorporate some of these practices into your daily life. If you want to return to a life of deep peace, happiness, joy and love, then these practices will help you find your way there. My suggestion is to start incorporating small changes into your daily routine, and as you notice yourself feeling better, you can add more practices to make long-lasting changes that align with your wholeness and the new person you're becoming.

The 5 Elements And Healing The Divine Body – The Tao Of Balance And Wholeness

The Tao literally translated is "The Way", a path to healing the physical body, and it consists of The 5 Elements: Wood, Fire, Earth, Metal and Water. The Tao is an ancient philosophy which consists of the natural balance found in nature and universal balance. It embodies the entire Universe and can be applied to the human physical body in natural healing using the 5 elements found in nature. Taoism honors the body as the temple for the spirit, which is why it's so effective in healing the physical body—it takes into consideration wholeness of the individual.

"In the past, people practiced the Tao, the Way of Life. They understood the principle of balance, of yin and yang, as presented by the transformation of the energies of the Universe. Thus they formulated practices such as Dao-in, an exercise combining stretching, massaging and breathing to promote energy flow and meditation to help maintain and harmonize themselves with the Universe. They ate a balanced diet at regular times, arose and retired at regular hours, avoided overstressing their bodies and minds and refrained from overindulgence of all kinds. They maintained well-being of body and mind: thus, it is not surprising that they lived over one hundred years."

"Yellow Emperor's Classic of Chinese Medicine."

When one is in emotional pain from grief or loss and the body is in an unbalanced state of being, it's wise to follow the Principles of the Tao to bring the body back into balance and back into the flow of life the natural way. Grieving can lead to depression, sadness or heartbreak which leads to an imbalance in the system. To restore balance, the natural response would be to cry and release the emotion, thus leading back to a balanced state. Don't you feel better after a good cry or release of pent up feelings in a healthy manner? Releasing the tears can be very healing. The way to heal is to feel and move through the emotion to the other side. One of the 6 myths of grief recovery is "Don't Feel Bad". I don't understand this one, because it truly denies the feelings and emotions associated with a loss. If I pretend I don't feel bad, then is it supposed to go away? Well, I'm here to tell you, that's a recipe for disaster. When you're unable or unwilling to express your feelings because you've been told by others not to feel bad, you bury these feelings and emotions in every cell of your body. This is the first stage of "dis-ease" which eventually turns into a disease of the body, mind or spirit. You MUST express and feel the feelings to release them. The only way to heal is to feel.

When following the Tao, you'll experience a state of happiness and joy that comes from achieving balance and harmony in the body, mind and spirit which includes deep inner peace, serenity, curiosity, tranquility and laughter. You will make great strides in your healing if you follow the principles and qualities of the 5 elements found in nature and align with the seasons of the year and the productive cycle of these 5 elements.

The 5 Elements Of Healing

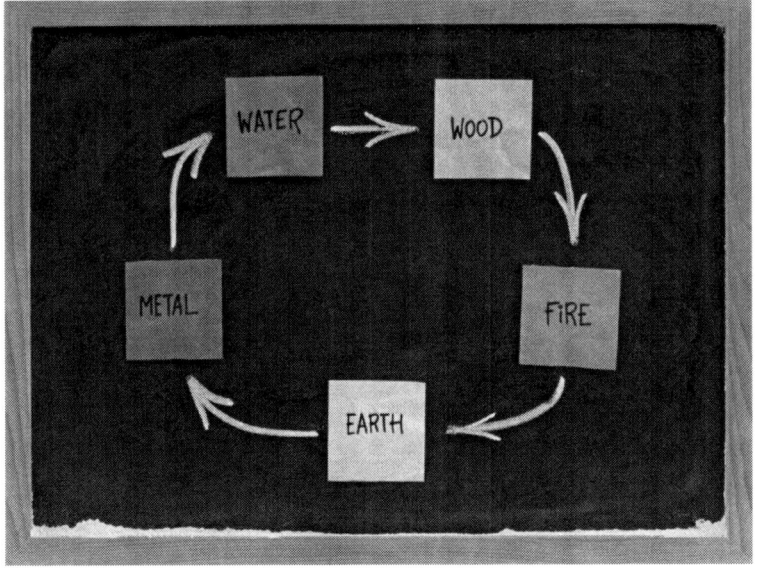

The 5 Elements Creative Cycle

The 5 elements maintain a balance of energies in the physical body as well as in all the Universe and nature. They have relationships for balance and harmony in the physical, emotional, mental and spiritual bodies. All of the 5 elements are within each individual as well as in the external world. However, each individual has a unique physical, emotional, mental and spiritual system. You can work with each of these elements and systems by being in the flow and not creating resistance which leads to imbalance. When you're experiencing the emotional pain of grief and loss, you're in an imbalanced state, and correction of the flow is in order to bring you back into balance.

The **Creative Cycle** consists of each element that creates the next element, so it's supporting that individual element. This is how it's explained:

Water on Wood makes Wood grow so it supports it in its growth.

Wood on Fire makes Fire larger so it supports it to grow.

Fire turns into Earth after it's burned and therefore makes Earth grow larger.

Earth creates Metal because metal is derived from the Earth so it creates more metal.

Metal creates water as in condensation so Metal creates Water.

And these 5 elements repeat their cycles over and over in the Creative Cycle of nature.

The 5 Elements Of Healing

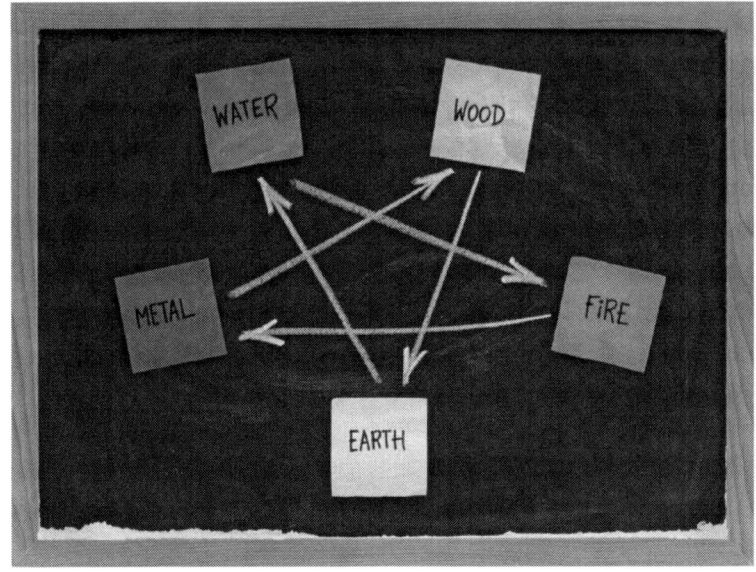

The 5 Elements Controlling Cycle

The **Controlling Cycle** of the 5 elements consists of the elements that are not supporting each other, and this is destructive to the energy system of the physical, emotional, mental and spiritual systems of the body. They're imbalanced and need correction when out of balance. This can happen in the external environment as well as the internal environment, so it's vital to balance both when working to overcome emotional pain due to grief and loss.

The Controlling Cycle consists of each element that controls the next element, so it's not supporting that individual element but depleting or destroying it. This is how it's explained:

Wood controls Earth by overtaking it .

Water controls Fire by putting fire out.

Metal controls Wood by chopping it.

Earth controls Water by absorption.

Fire controls Metal by melting it.

There's a beneficial use for both the creative cycle and the controlling cycle when working with the 5 elements of the internal and external environments. I'll discuss that when I go through each element on an individual basis. The main point here is to restore balance and harmony with these elements to create synergy between the physical, mental, emotional and the spiritual systems.

Now that you have seen how each of the 5 elements interrelate with each other in the creative and controlling cycles, let's take each element and see how you might use them in healing emotional pain due to grief and loss.

METAL ELEMENT
(ALSO KNOWN AS AIR ELEMENT IN SOME TRADITIONS)

In Chinese Traditional Medicine (CTM), the Metal Element represents the Autumn around the Autumn Equinox, and it signifies letting go and releasing what no longer serves you in your life. In the case of grief, you've already experienced the letting go and release of a person, pet, job or something you loved or was familiar to you—and lost. So, the acceptance of the loss and releasing of the emotional pain around the loss is what must take place to balance the Metal Element in the body. There may be other things in your life you must release and let go of now too, and this fits here in the element of Metal.

The Metal Element represents the lungs and the large intestine organs and meridians of the body. These relate to the elimination of oxygen through breathing and elimination of waste through the colon. The emotion associated with the Metal element is grief and sadness. Therefore, an imbalance in the Metal Element is a direct result of experiencing emotional pain due to grief and loss. So, we must look at the Metal Element within the context of the physical body to correct this imbalance through digestion and food—among other holistic practices that represent the Metal Element—to build up the Chi energy in the system combined with the Earth element. The Earth Element supports the Metal Element so it's useful in building up the Chi energy.

You can also look at other characteristics of the Metal Element to support yourself when experiencing emotional pain due to grief or loss such as:

1. Wearing the color white and surrounding your environment with the color white.

2. The sound of weeping or crying is a great release for the Metal Element.

3. Breathing exercises and meditations for the lungs.

4. Eating Autumn foods such as soup and root vegetables.

5. The sense organ for Metal Element is the nose, so aromatherapy is helpful.

6. Colonics or colon cleansing for elimination of waste.

7. Taking probiotics for digestive health and healing.

8. Releasing old emotions, attitudes and beliefs through various techniques.

"Letting go and letting God" is the motto here, and it's so important to begin releasing the old to make way for the new experiences coming your way. These are only a few holistic practices to help you in your time of grief and loss but a good start leading on your path to wholeness and happiness once again.

You can also work with the Metal Element through the Chakra system. Grief is tied to the second, fourth and fifth Chakras. So it's helpful to balance these Chakras when balancing the Metal Element within the physical body.

In the final chapter on Feng Shui for the mind, body and the spirit, I'll be offering suggestions on incorporating the Metal Element into your external environment to support you in healing your home, office or landscape for the total healing package. You'll see huge shifts in your life when balance is achieved in your internal and external worlds together for total peace and harmony.

Water Element

The Water Element represents the season of Winter around the Winter Solstice, the time of year when we experience the coldest season and most darkness, which represent the symbol for water. Water also represents the emotion of unconscious fears and the internal beliefs about what's happening in your world after experiencing a loss. This can be a very unpredictable time in your life where you have no control over your world. You know where you've been and you know where you are, but you have no clue where you're going next. You've lost someone or something you love. This creates great fear on the conscious as well as the unconscious level. All your past fears that are stored in cellular memory are presented to you as well in a time of uncertainty. This is a time when it's required that you surrender to the flow of your external and internal world and maintain stillness to balance the Water Element. It's the most crucial time to maintain your trust and faith as you listen to your inner wisdom and the Divine Intelligence to achieve overall well-being and balance the Water Element.

The Water Element represents the bladder and kidney organs and meridians. These are the water systems in our bodies and regulate flow through those organs. When the Water Element is balanced and strong, you have courage, motivation and endurance to achieve great things in life and to overcome your fears. However, if the bladder and the kidney are weak, then you have an imbalance and you're more inclined to be in fear. By working with the bladder and kidney meridians, the Chi energy is strengthened and balance is achieved. The Metal Element supports the Water Element, so all the holistic practices in the Metal Element section are useful for this element as well as those that are specifically for the Water Element.

You may want to incorporate the characteristics of the Water Element into your daily life to create balance and avoid weak Water Element in your constitution through these activities :

1. Wearing the color blue or black or having it in your environment.

2. Spending time in and around water influences such as lake, ocean, pools or spas.

3. Taking sea salt baths to detoxify and purify yourself.

4. Incorporating water fountains or fish tanks into your home or office.

5. The sense organ for the water element is the ear, so listening to soft music.

6. Listening to guided meditation recordings.

7. Drinking more water as in eight 8 oz. glasses of purified water a day.

8. Eating cooked, warm foods such as soups, stews, casseroles, beans and whole grains.

9. Doing Yoga for greater flexibility, body flow and meditation.

10. Meditation in stillness to reflect inward.

11. Regular sleep schedule with 8 hours or more.

12. Slowing down in life to go inward during this time to listen to the Divine flow.

13. Deep body therapy for release of deep emotional wounds in your cellular memory.

14. Releasing old emotions and fears through techniques such as Hypnosis, Neuro Linguistic Programming (NLP) and Emotional Freedom Technique (EFT).

15. Dancing is great such as Wu Tao Dance or your favorite type of dancing in the flow.

"Going with the flow" is the motto here, and it's so important to begin releasing your fears around moving forward to new experiences coming your way. You can incorporate these practices into your daily routine a little at a time until you're ready for more. You'll notice that you'll be led to the pathway of a peaceful heart once again with more love, compassion, joy and gratitude then you can imagine.

The Water Element can also be balanced through the Chakra energy system. The Chakras that are connected with fear are the first, third, fifth and sixth chakras. By working to balance each of these Chakras, you'll help maintain balance within the entire energy system returning you to wholeness, happiness and deep peace.

WOOD ELEMENT

The Wood Element is the next element in the creative cycle of creating balance and harmony within the physical body. The Wood Element represents the Spring around the Spring Equinox, the time of the year for new beginnings and growth. When you're experiencing the emotional pain of grief and loss, this element may have an imbalance due to the emotion of anger. Anger is the emotion for the Wood Element, and after a significant loss, anger is one of the stages of grief, and the danger—and the anger creates an imbalance in the Wood Element of the physical body.

You may or may not experience anger on your journey through grief and loss, but if you do then you must have the willingness to surrender, accept and forgive in order to transcend the negative emotion of anger. The healthy balanced Wood Element accepts the loss and moves forward to create a new start with a new vision of how you would like to move forward in your world. You start to use your creative self-expression towards growth of the new and exciting possibilities for life. There is life after loss and a greater purpose for you to move forward. The imbalance of the Wood energy is where people get stuck in a vicious cycle of being the victim and not moving ahead. There's blocked energy resulting in stagnation. To heal from this emotional pain, you must be willing to release the past and start a new path that may not be visible to you at the time. But by taking that one step forward, the next step will be revealed to you, and you're now moving forward on your journey. Each step you take will reveal more, and you must have the courage, faith and trust that you're being lead in the direction of your highest good.

The Wood Element represents the liver and gall bladder organs and meridians. The liver is the organ that stores the blood and maintains a smooth flow of Chi energy throughout the physical body. The eyes, muscles and nails are also associated with the Wood Element. When you experience the pain of loss, you may sometimes become addicted to substances to numb the emotional pain. This is considered a Wood imbalance, so it's necessary to balance the Wood Element to return to a healthy pattern of behavior. Most problems related to addiction are caused by a liver imbalance. Physical detoxifying and toning of the liver are helpful when treating addiction due to grief or loss. The Water Element supports the Wood Element in the creative cycle, so its holistic practices would also be helpful to balance the Wood Element.

You may want to incorporate the characteristics of the Wood Element into your daily life to avoid weak Wood Element in your body temple by taking this actions:

1. Wearing the color green or having it in your home.

2. Incorporating green healing plants into your environment.

3. Planting and spending time in the garden growing things.

4. Eating a light diet consisting of greens, fruits, nuts and seeds.

5. Doing a cleanse of the physical body or a specific liver cleanse.

6. The sense organ is the eyes, so doing creative visualizations.

7. Creating and visualizing how you want to live your new life.

8. Spending time in the woods hiking and exploring new areas.

9. Spending time in nature specifically meditating around trees.

10. Creating a vision board of the things you want to attract into your life.

11. Taking classes that move you towards personal growth.

12. Eliminating those things and people in your life that no longer serve you.

13. Starting a new exercise program that makes your heart sing.

14. Dancing or starting a new physical activity that you love.

"What you sow, you shall reap" is the motto for Wood Element, and it's helpful for you to release the emotion of anger and plant new seeds of growth to cultivate a new beginning in your life. You can release those unwanted addictions replacing them with your creative self-expression as you incorporate some of these activities into your day so you can live the life you want. You must believe it to see it show up in your life. Enjoy the journey and the process, for it's sometimes that road that brings us the best gifts in life, and not the final destination. Take time to smell the roses, and you'll find more happiness and wholeness in your life.

The Wood Element can also be balanced through the Chakra energy system to maintain balance and harmony in the body temple. The Chakras connected with anger are the first, fourth, fifth and sixth Chakras. By working to balance these 4 Chakras, you'll find a new balance of the Wood Element returning the entire energy system to wholeness, happiness and deep peace. I address the specific ways of the healing of the Chakras for each specific element in relation to grief and loss in my retreats and workshops. Please check out my healing retreats now if you're interested in knowing more about my process for healing grief at www.SandraRuggles.com.

THE FIRE ELEMENT

The Fire Element represents the season of Summer around the Summer Solstice, the time of year we experience the peak of sunlight and warm weather which is very symbolic of the Fire Element. It represents the emotion of Joy and the heart, and this is the outlet for your Spirit. It's the outward expression of the emotions, communication and action. You can imagine someone who's joyful will often express their joy through laughter, another attribute for the Fire Element. In grief, there's an absence of the Fire Element, because the opposite end of the spectrum of joy is sadness or grief. If you're experiencing the emotional pain of grief or loss, then it's essential to incorporate the Fire Element into your life. An imbalance in the Fire Element is hiding from the world, overeating and drinking and non-action or just not engaging in life. By simply adding some Fire Element to your life, you'll see a shift in your ability to be happier and feel whole.

The Fire Element represents transformation and purification, so this is a time for change, action and purifying your spirit to allow the transformation to take place in your heart. The organ for the Fire Element is the heart;

by following your heart, you'll merge with your spirit and flourish and grow to your true potential. By listening to your heart, you'll be in joy and you'll uncover your purpose and passions to live life to its fullest. The tongue and communication are also attributes of the Fire Element. "Speak your truth" and actively communicate to those around you what you're feeling during times of your emotional pain. Don't hold everything inside, because this would be an imbalance in the Fire Element. If you can't talk to your immediate family and friends, then find a coach or a support group of other like-minded souls who you trust to speak openly with about your feelings, thoughts and emotions. This will help you to heal yourself quickly and you'll even make some new friends.

At times of great change as grieving the loss of a person or a job, you'll find that you'll release some of your old friends and even some family members who can't support you through this hard time. It's not that they don't love you or they don't care, but they have their own issues about grief and loss and possibly don't understand how to support another. You're outside their comfort zone and they can't adjust to you. So, let them go and move forward surrounding yourself with a support system of people who can weather this storm with you. They're the ones who have "been there, done that" or are living the life you want to move to next. It's all right to let people go while you're adjusting to your new life. It's normal and healthy to maintain self-love and boundaries during this time of great change. Communication is the key to balancing the Fire Element in your life.

The Fire Element represents the organs and meridians of the heart and small intestine. Living with a healthy heart is the key to longevity and a healthy life. When the heart is in balance, you have vitality, creativity, love and abundant health. When the heart is not in balance, it can lead to "dis-ease" or death. So, it would be wise to incorporate as much Fire Element into your life as possible to maintain a happy and healthy existence. The small intestine is responsible for digestion and determining what will be released and what will be held in the body for nutrition. A healthy digestion of food and thoughts will keep the Fire Element in balance. I've heard that the small and large intestine, the stomach and the esophagus are the Intestinal Brain—one of three brains located in the physical body. The other two brains are in the heart as in the "Heart Brain" and the "Head Brain". So the "Intestinal Brain" gives you signals about your emotions and your "gut instincts". Pay attention to those "gut instincts" and you'll use this brain to its full potential. By following your heart in all areas of your life, you'll be following your "Heart Brain" and the secret to a long and happy life.

There are 2 additional meridians not recognized in Western medicine, but these are recognized in Traditional Chinese Medicine. They are the Pericardium (The Protector of the Heart) and the Triple Heater which regulates the heat and energy for the body. Providing circulation and heating to the body through this Fire Element keeps the body in harmony with abundant health.

You may want to incorporate the characteristics of the Fire Element into your daily life to avoid weak Fire Element in your constitution and create balance and harmony through these activities:

1. Wearing the color red as this represents the Fire Element.

2. Decorating your home with the color red is the Fire Element.

3. Getting plenty of sunshine and light to enhance the Fire Element.

4. Getting plenty of aerobic type exercise to strengthen the heart.

5. Connect with your spirit daily through meditation and prayer.

6. Meditating with red candles that represent the Fire Element.

7. Connecting with what makes you joyful daily.

8. Taking time to laugh every day and see the humor in life.

9. Eating light summer foods such as salads, vegetables, nuts and fruits.

10. Taking action on your ideas gained through the Wood Element.

11. Communicating with like-minded friends and family for support.

12. Speaking your truth about your purpose and passions.

13. Getting outside in nature and staying active.

14. Connecting with animals and pets as they represent the Fire Element.

"Get To The Heart of the Matter" and "Light My Fire" are two mottos that represent the Fire Element that pretty much explain a balance of the Fire Element. You can begin to incorporate these practices into your daily routine a little at a time until you're ready for more. You'll see your life kick into action by incorporating Fire into your life after loss.

The Fire Element can also be balanced through the Chakra energy system. The Chakras connected with the emotion of joy are the fourth, sixth and seventh Chakras. By balancing the Heart Chakra, Third Eye Chakra and the Crown Chakra you can remedy the Fire imbalance and all is well once again. So, when in doubt, go to your heart and connect it with your intuition and the divine source and you'll find all your answers there just waiting for you.

Earth Element

The Earth Element represents the season of Late Summer before Autumn begins, which is the time of year that the weather is changing, school begins and people are typically getting ready for the colder weather. The emotion associated with the Earth Element is Sympathy. So, this is quite fitting for someone going through the

emotional pain of grief and loss. This is a time to grieve, and it's healthy to acknowledge the loss and move through it. The Earth Element also represents balance which should be done in a balanced way of feeling sympathy while moving forward in a healthy manner. The Earth Element is about thinking and thoughts, so this would be a time to ground and center your thoughts in a healthy way. Keep your thoughts positive and avoid dwelling on the grief. The best way to achieve this is by being still and relaxed, spending time in meditation. You're preparing for change, so ground yourself in Mother Earth sitting or walking in nature to balance the Earth Element. This element will help you manifest new ideas, new thoughts and a new life if you keep yourself in balance in all things. Singing is the sound of the Earth Element, so it would be helpful to sing to your favorite songs that make you feel much better. If you don't sing, then just hum to the music, and you'll find your vibrational frequency will raise with just a little bit of toning to music. The smell for the Earth Element are fragrances, so indulge yourself with fresh flowers, aromatherapy and whatever smells beautiful. This will change your environment by including the Earth Element in a most pleasing way.

The Earth Element represents the stomach and spleen organs and meridians, so it's no wonder that the sense organ is the mouth. This is where you want to place your focus—on all you take in and digest as nourishment for your physical body, mind and spirit. So, you may want to take a look at how you're nourishing yourself through all the changes in your life due to your loss. You may be having problems with food or digestion, and this would represent an Earth imbalance. It's time to eat organic, healthy foods and be conscious of your eating decisions. The taste for the Earth Element is sweetness, so include healthy and organic sweet foods in your diet and remember to maintain balance in all your food choices. By eliminating sugar from your diet and substituting with honey or Stevia, you'll be making a healthier choice. Stevia is a plant fiber that's good for your body as opposed to refined sugar which is toxic to the physical body. Keep the Earth Element balanced to maintain a healthy body, mind and spirit.

You may want to incorporate the characteristics of the Earth element into your daily life to avoid weak Earth Element in your constitution and create balance and harmony through these choices:

1. Wearing the color yellow or earth tones.

2. Decorating your home with earth tones, plants and crystals for Earth Element.

3. Spending time in a flower or vegetable garden.

4. Taking nature walks to get grounded and centered.

5. Meditating and deep breathing outside in nature.

6. Singing to your favorite music.

7. Eating lighter foods easier on the stomach and digestion such as fruits, vegetables, fish, chicken, whole grains, beans, lentils and brown rice.

8. Taking probiotics to enhance digestion.

9. Eating 5 small meals instead of larger intakes of food at one time.

10. Removing sugar from your diet and substituting Stevia.

11. Being conscious of your thoughts and remembering to surrender to life's changes.

12. Using essential oils and aromatherapy to enhance your life.

13. Remembering to maintain balance in all things in your life.

14. Preparing for your new beginning and having faith that all things are working out for your highest good.

"Don't lose your ground" is the motto here, and you want to maintain your ground, center and balance with the Earth Element. The emotion of sympathy is only there to acknowledge the grief, but you don't want to wallow in your sympathy or use it as a means to escape from life. You can begin to incorporate these practices into your daily life a little at a time until you're ready to make bigger changes. You'll move closer to your peaceful heart and you'll find self-love, happiness, joy and peace.

The Earth Element can be balanced through the Chakra energy system. The Chakras connected with sympathy are the second, third, fourth, fifth and seventh. By working to balance each of these Chakras, you'll maintain balance within the entire energy system returning you to wholeness.

Acupressure For Grief And Loss

One of the techniques I've used for healing the physical body from the emotional pain of grief and loss is self-administering Acupressure points specifically for grief, depression and emotional balancing. By placing your fingertips on specific points to release the blocked energy, you'll feel much better as you create a powerful energy flow. This works incredibly for emotional balancing of the human energy system, and specifically for grief. You'll find videos on my website indicating exactly where the acupressure points are located so you can self-administer for proper placement of points and enjoy a most rewarding experience.

What I have found to be even more effective is adding essential oils to the points as you're pressing on them. In this way, you can expand the benefits received from that point by adding specific essential oils. The aromatherapy oils are named for their benefit: Release, Harmony, Forgiveness, Surrender, Joy, Transformation, Gratitude, Hope and Peace & Calming. You can purchase these and more essential oils from my website at www.SandraRuggles.com.

Yoga

I wanted to include my appreciation for the practice of Yoga in my healing journey to wholeness. I started doing yoga as a regular practice while going through a lot of emotional pain due to my grief and loss and found it to be quite healing. It wasn't a practice I could do well at first, but over the years, I found a correlation between how I felt when I did yoga and how I felt when I didn't do yoga. I felt a renewed sense of life and confidence when I did a regular yoga practice of at least 3 times a week.

I once heard T.Harv Eker say, "How you do one thing is how you do everything." I really began to see the parallels in my life with how I was doing my yoga postures. When I'm doing a posture in a beautiful correct stance or position, I feel so empowered. And that's a lot like life— when you're very good at something, you feel great. When I couldn't do a posture or it was half way right, I noticed how those feelings and emotions filtered into my life. Did I give it my all? What was I fearful of? Did I force it to happen? I started making these interesting correlations between my yoga practice and my life. I started changing my thoughts and actions to become more effective in all areas of my life. And I had a new awareness of my fears and where I got stuck. I realized the thoughts behind the behaviors which gave me the courage to make the necessary changes. So, my yoga practice really helped me in my self-realization of how I was living my life in all areas. It brought me self-love in ways I could never have imagined and it moved me closer to the Divine.

I would like to suggest beginning a yoga practice to enhance your emotional healing and derive the physical benefits of balance, strength and flexibility. You'll experience the gratifying result of a healthy body, mind and spirit.

Wu Tao Dance – Dance Yourself To Health

I want to include Wu Tao Dance in my discussion on physical healing of the body, mind and spirit, because I've found this to be an amazing addition to my healing. When I heard about Wu Tao "The Dancing Way", I knew immediately I wanted to incorporate this into my daily practice. I've been doing Wu Tao for about 3 months now and have found it to be a wonderful addition to my health and healing. So much so that I must include it as a healing therapy for the mind, body and spirit.

What is Wu Tao Dance? It's a combination of dance moves and stretches that help restore balance to the body and harmonize the flow of life force energy known as Chi. It also includes healing the body in a joyful, playful way that results in a renewed sense of being. Wu Tao involves dancing, moving the body, music, stillness, meditation and contemplation. It's highly creative and has huge health benefits, because it balances the organs and the meridian channels of the body according to the 5 elements. There's a dance for each element: Fire Element Dance, Earth Element Dance, Air Element Dance, Water Element Dance and Wood Element Dance. This style of dance is based on Traditional Chinese Medicine and utilizes the foundations of its teachings. In Traditional Chinese Medicine, the Air Element is sometimes used as the Metal Element, so these are used interchangeably. Your dancing allows for expressive emotional, mental and spiritual release while moving and listening to the music. Your body, mind and spirit are transformed, returning you to balance, peace and centeredness. Wu Tao is the ultimate stress management system. As you do the dances and the energy is moved through your body, your mind and emotions are cleared and balanced with a renewed sense of peace. This is so healing for those experiencing the painful emotions of grief and loss as it clears your energy blocks so you can be free to begin a new way of living life.

Wu Tao Dance is for all ages and is easy to learn. You can learn more by going to www.WuTaoDance.com. Michelle Locke, the creator and founder of Wu Tao Dance, is from Western Australia and is an inspiring educator, passionate dancer, and dedicated to improving the physical and spiritual health of people everywhere. Read more about Wu Tao Dance and Michelle Locke by going to her website.

I've shared many techniques in this chapter on Healing For The Divine Physical Body to Unlock The Grief Code. I'm sure you've gained some valuable ideas and tools to help you move forward from your emotional pain due to grief and loss on your path towards wholeness, happiness and peace of mind.

Unlocking The Grief Code – Aligning With Spirit For Healing

"Everyone sees the unseen in proportion to the clarity of his heart, and that depends upon how much he has polished it. Whoever has polished it sees more-more unseen forms become manifest to him."

—*Rumi*

THIS IS THE MOST IMPORTANT piece of the healing process that connects us into our Oneness to all. When the spirit aligns with the mind and body there's a connection that's transcending. You are way beyond the physical limitations, and you can see with your spiritual eyes of pure unconditional love, acceptance, forgiveness and surrender. You now recognize that in the loss that you are facing and the resulting challenges and conflicts you are experiencing that there's a blessing somewhere in all of this, and it's moving you deeper into evolving your soul. You surrender the struggle and all the resistance to allow Spirit to move and guide you towards your future destination. Spirit always knows the way even if you don't know the way.

The question then becomes what is the connection between the soul and spirit? This is a hard distinction to determine, but here is a relatively simple way to explain it as it was explained to me. When aligning with our spirit, we're aligning with our higher self which connects the soul with the physical body. Aligning with Spirit affects the human energy system and the energetic frequencies and energy patterns that we emanate and attract into our life based on the soul's intentions for this incarnation. The soul is what animates the physical body and stores all memories from your birth to your death in this lifetime and other past lifetimes. When the soul leaves the physical body at the time of death, then the physical body uses the spirit as a vehicle to exit and transition from the physical back into energy.

During a time of grief or loss, we can sometimes feel separated from our spirit or our very soul, although that can never happen in truth. This results in those feelings of frustration, anger, fear, heartbreak and grief. We're in the struggle of life and in resistance to change. This is when it's useful to use the tools and techniques within this chapter to get back in alignment with your spirit and your soul. You'll be coming home to yourself when you begin to notice that you're in alignment with your spirit and your soul.

There are many ways to align with Spirit, and here are a few to begin with:

1. Meditation to align with Spirit.

2. Affirmative Prayer or Spiritual Mind Treatment.

3. Intuition Development.

4. Being in Nature.

5. Ceremony and Rituals.

6. Creating Altars and Sacred Space.

7. Community with like-minded people

8. Attending a Spiritual Center or Place of Worship regularly.

Meditation for Aligning with Spirit

Meditation for aligning with Spirit consists of connecting with your higher self to listen for guidance from the Divine Intelligence or God. This is allowing yourself to be open and receptive to listen to the thoughts, words, symbols, pictures, sounds, smells and all the subtle energy around you. I would suggest asking a question, writing it down and then going into a 20-minute meditation seeking clarity, guidance and wisdom. Bring a notepad with you so you can begin writing down the answers to your questions that may have surfaced during your meditation. If you begin writing down whatever comes to mind, you will begin to get into the flow of the energy, and the writing will become easy and effortless for the answers you're seeking.

Meditation for aligning with Spirit is also taking proper care of the human energy system. When the human energy system is clear without any energy blocks, illness or disease then it's free flowing creating a high vibration or frequency. All is well and the mind, body and spirit are integrated. The human energy system is a barometer of your emotional, mental, physical and spiritual health. During times of grief or loss, the human energy system should be treated with love and compassion to nurture all components back to balance. The meditation for aligning with Spirit is be open and allow Spirit to flow through your human energy system purging you of all that no longer serves you and replacing with self-love, deep peace and joy. You'll find the Chakra Meditation in chapter 4 to be one that would help you in the aligning with your spirit. You can make up your own or just sit in silence allowing Spirit to return you to your wholeness once again experiencing love, joy, peace and compassion.

There are many other meditations for aligning with your spirit that may be from your religious tradition or you have a personal preference to continue with, so do what feels right for you. It's important to recognize here that taking time each day to align with your spirit in a very personal way such as meditation will change your life. Your emotional pain from the grief and loss will lessen, and you'll find the deep peace and the unconditional love you've been seeking.

AFFIRMATIVE PRAYER OR SPIRITUAL MIND TREATMENT

This is a positive prayer that comes from a spiritual philosophy called Science of Mind. It's based on the writings of Dr. Ernest Holmes who stated that the essence of truth is in all religions. He took the spiritual truths and created the philosophy of Science of Mind.

The Affirmative Prayer or Spiritual Mind Treatment can be done for any type of problem, illness or to release your grief through forgiveness, acceptance and surrender. I have included Spiritual Mind Treatments written by Connie Vaughn in chapters 2 and 3 which address Surrender, Acceptance and Foregiveness. Please feel free to use these to align with Spirit, or you can create your own by following a 5-step process. You can ask for good health, wealth, a job, relationships or anything you desire to come into your reality. Then just use this format to declare the following and use this process for affirmative prayer.

1. Recognition – You state that "God IS". You proclaim that God exists here and there is nowhere where God is not.

2. Unification – You state "I AM". You open your heart and mind to the Divine God-consciousness. Release limitations in thinking and merge with the Divine Presence allowing the one mind to be revealed in your own mind.

3. Realization – You state "I KNOW". You know this to be the truth of your being. You absolutely know without a doubt that this Spiritual Law creates a result according to your belief.

4. Thanksgiving – You state "IT IS SO". You express gratitude and thanks for knowing that your desired result has been already fulfilled.

5. Release – You state "I LET GO LET GOD". As you let go, you let the activity of Spirit unfold, and you know that this is for the highest good of all. Spirit always leads you in the direction of truth, happiness and love.

You can write your own prayer by following this 5-step process for yourself or for others who you would like to pray for too. Just put in your desired prayer with your own words following the format. You'll love the results when you put this into your spiritual practice daily.

Intuition Development

Developing your intuition will shift you in alignment with your spirit because these are one in the same. Your intuition is the path to your wisdom, your guidance and that inner knowing that you know you must follow. There's a certainty that comes with those intuitive ideas and thoughts when you experience those flashes of insight and you're confident that this is true information. This is aligning you with our spirit at the same time you're receiving the gift of intuition.

In times of emotional pain due to grief and loss, you may at times feel disconnected from your intuition and your sixth sense. It's important to recognize that you can shift right back into your intuitive mind at any time you desire. You can put into practice a few of these suggestions, and then you'll be able to exercise your intuition muscle to fine-tune it and use it more in your life for decision-making or problem-solving activities.

Here a few suggestions for developing your intuition:

1. Pay attention to first impressions and those "Aha" moments.

2. Honor those flashes and hunches that seem to come out of nowhere.

3. Your body is talking to you. Pay attention to what your body is telling you.

4. Intuition speaks in symbols, pictures and images, so begin to notice patterns.

5. Relaxation and Meditation are used to enhance intuition.

6. Write down your intuitive hunches and inspiration to refer to for answers.

7. Pay attention to the subtle whispers as these can be subtle nudges to change.

8. Your intuition should empower not disempower you.

9. Spiritual intuition is internal not external.

These are just a few suggestions for intuition development to align with Spirit in your life as you move out of the dark night of emotional pain due to grief and loss and into the light of Spirit that awaits your return.

Being In Nature

One of the most healing retreats of all is being out in nature. In nature this is where you can really align with Spirit and more…and nurture yourself in the 5 elements of healing.

Hiking or walking through the woods is associated with the wood element. Take a hike or a walk to explore nature trails in your area to enjoy the natural beauty and connect with Spirit.

A trip to the ocean is a great way to gather all the positive ions from the salt water mist. The energy of the ocean environment carries the elements of fire, earth, water, wood and metal.

You may be at your home in your backyard or in nature somewhere in your local area.

The location must be one that brings you a sense of contentment, peace and unconditional love. When you find that special place in nature, then you have found a spot where you can go whenever you want to connect with Spirit. This is a place of self-love that's just for you.

If you can't be outside in nature due to weather conditions, then bring nature inside your home. Create an environment for live plants, flowers and herbs inside the house that will bring nature inside. This can also be incorporating water fountains and pictures of nature too. Mirrors reflecting windows and doors will also bring the outside inside a room for that look and feel of being in nature. Create an indoor sanctuary to connect with Spirit and bring nature inside.

Ceremonies And Rituals

Our culture teaches us the traditions of ceremonies and rituals within our lives. All of us have gone through these ceremonies and rituals of life: birthdays, holidays, graduations, marriages, anniversaries, significant achievements, death and spiritual events. We share these with other people, and it creates a declaration to the world that our life or the lives of our loved ones are honored and celebrated. However, when we experience a loss of a loved one or a loss of a situation, then our lives will change in the way we connect with others. We oftentimes will feel the emotional pain and grieve more during significant dates such as birthdays, holidays, anniversaries and celebrations of any kind. It's during these days that it's important to become conscious of our alignment with Spirit to let go of the pain and allow spirit to guide us through this time.

What is the difference between a ceremony and a ritual? A ritual is an action that's performed for symbolic value. A ritual is performed at a ceremony or on a specific occasion. A ritual can be done individually or with a group of people. A ceremony is an event that includes rituals performed for significant life happenings and rites of passage. That's the difference between a ritual and ceremony.

I bring this to your attention because you'll find when in emotional pain due to grief and loss, the ceremonies that come up day after day, year after year will not change. These are ceremonies that can't be avoided because they're a part of our very culture. Although these may be hard for you the first year or two after the loss, the rituals associated with these ceremonies are totally up to you and your happiness. The rituals are the one way you can shift your consciousness to align with Spirit during these challenging times.

When you're conscious of the thoughts that you're thinking, then you can create magic for yourself during the holidays or during yearly ceremonies. These ceremonies are not the same as in the past and someone or something is missing; you feel alone and your thoughts are "stuck" in the past and the way life used to be. Welcome this opportunity to align with Spirit and ask yourself the following questions:

1. How can I honor my loss in a new and different way this year? A new ritual?

2. Who can serve as my support system during this holiday season or during the ceremony?

3. Who do I need to forgive including myself to feel better?

4. How can I have complete acceptance of what has happened to move through this?

5. What do I have control over in my life, and how can I change what I can control?

By getting still in meditation and asking yourself some simple questions, you can shift your thinking to one of being empowered which leads to unlocking the grief code within you and puts you on your pathway to the peaceful heart.

The heart of healing is through the mind, body and spirit. However, I don't know many that have healed from grief and loss without awareness of the spiritual path to healing. Seek out a spiritual outlet in your own faith tradition that can help you commemorate the "deeper reason" for the ceremony or ritual. This will allow you to have a deeper meaning and purpose in your life.

You may want to incorporate some of these "tools for the spirit" in your life during this time of ceremony or a holiday season to help you move through your heartbreak and emotional pain shifting to peace of mind, love and joy once again:

1. Find the Spirituality area of your home (in the South) and create an altar there for yourself or your loved one so you have a place to get away from life and connect with either yourself or them there for comfort. This can include photos, symbols, candles, scents or anything that represents your loved one or the new life you would like to create in the present moment.

2. Incorporate a balance of meditation and prayer in your day to ask for guidance towards healing, and then listen for the answers. Write the answers in a journal.

3. Create a journal for healing the spirit in which you spend time daily writing those things that are connecting you with the Divine through your daily blessings. Write about the person, place or situation you have lost in your life and what you are truly grateful for about the other person, place or situation and the good memories.

4. Pay attention to the signs and synchronicities from the angelic realm and your higher power as to your next baby step towards healing. Sometimes, this is revealed moment by moment and

day by day, so be patient and allow for divine timing to take place without forcing things to happen.

5. Plant a small tree, flowers, plants or anything that will grow and flourish in honor of your loved one, and decorate and water with intention to connect with joyful memories. This can also be done for those creating a new life after loss of a career, job or home. You're growing a new life, so it's beautiful when it's symbolized with a real life-giving symbol.

6. Add a new pet to your family as this will bring you comfort and companionship.

7. Visit a spiritual site somewhere in the world, and get away from daily life during these times of ceremony. It's alright to do things differently now and create a new ritual during times of holidays and other ceremonies.

8. Volunteer to assist others who are experiencing the same loss so you can support each other during these times.

These are just a few suggestions for connecting and aligning with Spirit for healing. There are many rituals that can be done for healing grief and loss which are too numerous to mention in this book, but join my workshops and retreats to experience the many ways to align with Spirit.

Creating Altars And Sacred Space

It's so important to create sacred space away from the outside world into your home so that you can have a sanctuary to align with Spirit in a very intimate and individual way. Your home should represent a sanctuary from the outside world to bring peace and happiness to you. This space will serve and represent the way you think and feel about yourself and your loved ones. It may be that you have lost someone in the home or a situation surrounding your home, in which case creating a sacred space in your home becomes the healing ground for your recovery. If you are under stress or depressed due to your grief and loss, it's important to create a place you can release from the stress and feel safe and secure from the world to align with your spirit. You'll find that when you align with Spirit, you'll feel happier and at peace once again. Therefore, you're creating your own healing environment to recover in the quickest time possible.

According to Classical Feng Shui design and placement, there are auspicious placements for a sanctuary, sacred space and an altar inside the home. The South is known as the "Spirituality area," so it would be beneficial to have your sacred space or altar in the South if possible. However, it can get more specific with additional personal information about the house and the occupants. Due to the changing influences yearly, monthly, daily and hourly of the cosmology of the Universe, there may be other areas that are more powerful in your home. In order to locate the best placement for your sanctuary, sacred space or altar, it's better to consult with a professional Feng Shui Practitioner to determine the best placement in your home. The site analysis is based on the occupant's birth information, the yearly influences, placement and age of the home. You can contact me at www.SandraRuggles.com to order your personalized assessment for your home.

There are certain elements to introduce into a home or a space that can help create a sacred healing environment. These certain elements help to hold the vibration to the highest level possible to assist the healing process of the occupant who is in need of aligning with Spirit and healing from the emotional pain of grief and loss. In addition to using good Feng Shui design within the home to bring balance and harmony to all areas within, some additional remedies can be added to insure a sanctuary is created. Here are some suggestions:

1. ***Sacred Objects*** – Place objects such as a special deity that you pray to, a spiritual leader, statuary, crystals, bells, chimes, feathers, photographs and incense within your sacred space. Use these items on an altar or just place each one appropriately

in an area to infuse power from the spiritual realm allowing you to align with Spirit. You can use these sacred objects by creating a daily ritual with prayer and meditation to align with Spirit.

2. ***Books or Spiritual Guidance Tools*** – It's helpful to be reading spiritual books and magazines, listening to healing audio tapes and watching spiritual movies and media. This will help you in seeking higher wisdom, guidance and healing. It's helpful to have spiritual guidance tools in your sacred space as well like positive affirmation cards, pendulum, music or guided imagery CDs or any oracles that help with connecting with God or the Divine, your spiritual guides, angels and the universal consciousness.

3. ***Life Force Energy*** – This can be plants, flowers, fish tanks, water fountains, animals and pets, musical instruments and wind chimes.

4. ***Color*** – All color has a vibration and resonates to a frequency that heals the body or activates the body in some way. I will be including information on color healing in Chapter 10, the final chapter, so you may see how each color affects your biology on a subtle level.

5. ***Create An Altar*** – This can be a space set aside to place objects that have special meaning to you. I recommend placing an altar in your sacred space for meditation and prayer.

6. ***Regular Blessing Ceremonies*** – This is a good habit to practice on a regular basis in the home. This can be done at the full moon, during a new moon, a solstice or after an illness or conflict. You can use sage, incense, essential oils or candles to burn during the blessing ceremony to purify the energy of the space. Then say a prayer, affirmation or mantra as you're burning the sage, incense, essential oils or candles. This will bless your sacred space and cleanse and purify the energy in the space. I recommend a sacred ancient

method of clearing energy in any home or room using the method known as "Tracing the Nine Star Path". This is a Feng Shui cure taught by the late Grand Master Professor Lin Yun. If you would like to know more about this method of clearing energy in a home, office or landscape, please go to my website www.SandraRuggles.com and you can download the recording with step-by-step instructions for you to use in your sacred space.

In conclusion, creating a sacred space within your home is also creating a sacred space within yourself. The outer environment of the home is a mirror reflection of what's inside you. For optimal healing, use Feng Shui design to create a beautiful, pleasing, sacred space within your home. The reward of using Feng Shui design is to create vibrant health and rapid healing within the body, mind and spirit. We all have the ability to heal ourselves by tapping into our higher power. By doing so, we're co-creating our home environment with the Divine Intelligence and the highest vibrational frequencies of the visible and invisible energies of this planet.

Community With Like-Minded People

The community that you surround yourself with while experiencing grief and loss is very important. It's important that you find a community of like-minded people who understand what you're going through and are willing to support you through this transition and transformative time. Those who you have relied on or associated with prior to your loss may not be the same community of people who you'll associate with in the present and the future. As you change, grow and evolve, new people, places and situations will show up in your life to support the person you are now or you are becoming. When you can be with a community of people who love and support you, you'll align with your spirit more fully as you'll feel more love and compassion for yourself and others. Your community will act as your mirror and reflect back to you all the love and compassion you need to heal your pain due to the grief and loss.

I felt this way when I entered the Grief Coach Academy and started my training as a Grief Recovery Coach with others who had experienced a life-shattering loss or two or three. I was in a room with a community of other Grief Coaches in training who understood the pain, the struggle, the identity crisis and all the emotions that I knew and was experiencing. We came together to help and support one another to release our own grief and then to help others relieve their grief. I felt at home with the other people who knew what it was like to experience the death of a spouse, a loss of a child or grandchild and how to live through it and heal it with grace and dignity. This was a community of like-minded people who were able to show me how to heal my pain as they were healing their pain. This community was priceless and contributed greatly to my healing in a much quicker, easier and softer way. You may need to seek out this community or you may want to join our community, but find a community that you can connect with and align your spirit in union with the others who share your same values, beliefs and lifestyle.

Please don't do this alone. It's best to work through grief and loss with a support system. You must surround yourself with a community who understands what you're going through, who will support you through the challenges of rebuilding your life again and share the wisdom of grief recovery. You may join our community by going to www.SandraRuggles.com and sign up to become a member and begin connecting with other like-minded people who will help support you through this time in your life.

Attending A Spiritual Center Or Place Of Worship Regularly

This chapter on aligning with spirit would not be complete without including the importance of attending a spiritual center or place of worship regularly. I recommend that you find a spiritual community with spiritual food for your soul. If you're not particularly religious and don't have a particular faith, there are many interfaith churches out there that accept everyone. However, if you're already affiliated with a certain religion, then it's wise to plug into the community of that church for support. There are many churches that have some kind of grief support for their congregation. Sometimes those in grief find it necessary to change their place of worship and start an entirely new practice, because it facilitates the alignment of Spirit and the Divine in a more profound way for them. Whatever your situation, you'll find that your grief will be relieved and your spiritual life will evolve by attending some type of a spiritual center or place of worship as soon as you feel ready for it. I recommend the sooner the better.

This concludes the chapter on Aligning the Spirit for Healing, and I hope this chapter has given you a few useful ideas to incorporate into your daily life. If you're experiencing the emotional pain of grief and loss, it would be wise to add one or two of these practices into your day and week. You'll begin to notice that by setting this intention to work on your spirit that you'll begin to release the pain and grief and shift to peace, happiness and love. When you align your spirit with the Divine, anything is possible. May you enjoy this Divine union!

This concludes the section on Healing the Mind, Body and Spirit, and I hope you have learned many new practices and ideas to set in motion in your life for healing the emotional pain of grief and loss. By working with all 3 in the holistic model of healing, you'll find that you will heal your grief faster and easier than working with 1 of the 3, or worse yet, doing nothing and waiting for time to pass. Remember, grief doesn't have to take a long time to heal with the right action steps.

Now that I have outlined all the Mind, Body and Spirit Healing "Soul"utions for Unlocking The Grief Code, I would like to begin my next section of this book on your new beginning. The next 3 chapters will be about moving forward in your life and incorporating wholeness, purpose, passion, pleasure and Feng Shui for healing into your life. How do you do that? You create a roadmap to your happiness. It's the roadmap from where you are right now to where you want to be that will get you there. This is your pathway to the peaceful heart.

Are you ready for a new beginning and a life filled with peace, joy, love and more beauty than you could imagine? Well, let's move forward on your road to wholeness.

Chapter 8

Your New Beginning – Your Roadmap To Wholeness

"Be really whole and all things will come to you."

—*Lao Tzu*

LET'S EXPLORE THE ROAD TO wholeness. What is wholeness? Are you whole? Yes, you are! Let me explain. If you knew what being a whole person was before reading this, you would already be that person, and allow me to tell you that you are already a whole being. If you didn't know that, like I didn't know that, then that's the missing piece to your happiness. Being a whole person is being someone who lacks nothing, and you have everything you need inside of you. You don't depend on your external circumstances, situations, losses or anything outside of yourself to make you happy. Happiness is an inside job. There was an extensive study done on what makes people happy, and the studies revealed that 40% of happiness is derived from recognizing and becoming aware of what's under your direct control in life. The study also revealed that 50% of the participants were happy due to choices they made and their habits. The study revealed that only 10% of happiness was due to external circumstances. What that means is that if you focus on 90% of what you have control over in your life, then only 10% of your happiness comes from the external circumstances. Does that get you excited? It should. It means implementing better choices and making every choice matter in your daily life can shift you and your life in ways that are simply magical.

Constructing your roadmap to wholeness will take you on a journey of self-discovery that could take hours, weeks or months. If you do it on your own, it could take months. If you follow the roadmap in this book or work with a coach, it will take less time. The question I have for you is how long do you want to wait to really be happy with a renewed sense of purpose and passion in life? It's time to get focused and become increasingly aware about yourself and what will move you forward in life. So let's begin where you are right now by asking yourself some questions about the major areas within your life:

MAJOR LIFE AREAS

I would like you to start where you are right now and describe your current reality in each of the following areas:

1. *Your Health and Self Care* – What is your current health status and your daily self-care habits?

2. *Your Relationship with your spouse, significant other and children, if any* – How are your relationships at this time?

3. *Your Life Path or Career* – What is your current life path or career?

4. *Your Family and Ancestors* – Who is your family? How would you describe them and your ancestors?

5. *Your Wealth and Finances* – What is your current financial status? Describe your current reality.

6. *Your Benefactors and Support Systems in life* – Who are the people who currently help you and are a support system in your life?

7. ***Your Spirituality or Connection to God*** – What is your current path of your spirituality?

8. ***Your Self-cultivation, Knowledge and Wisdom*** – What is your current state of personal growth and evolving through knowledge, education and inner wisdom?

Simply state the facts and when answering these questions, leave out judgments or emotions about these facts. When you have answered these questions and addressed all the above life areas, then you'll become aware of your current reality. You'll become aware of the way your thoughts are then showing up in your external world. This is the beginning point where you'll become aware of your current reality. It's important to write it down, so you can refer to it later down the road. Once we know where we are and where we want to go, then we can implement the changes towards our destination.

Creating Your Personal Vision Statement

The next step is to take the same questions and describe what you would love to be, do and have in all of these life areas. If I could wave a magic wand and give you anything that you have ever dreamed of, what would you create in each of these 8 life areas? If you could have the life of your dreams, how would you describe that vision? Make the vision really big without any limitations.

What we'll create here is your own personal Vision Statement. Use your imagination and become the imaginer of your life. It's best to write your vision statement in the present tense as if it's happening now, not in the future. Your current reality has no bearing on your vision statement, so don't let your current circumstances affect your future vision. Sometimes our greatest pain and unhappiness is to show us what we don't want in our life anymore, and now it's time to rephrase that to what we do want in our life. It's important that you be very specific with your vision. There's a universal law called the Power of Specificity, and being very specific with our dreams and visions will allow the Universe to understand completely what we want to create and bring into our world.

Determine Your Core Values

It's important to determine your core values while writing your vision statement. It's your values that determine how you'll live your life and spend a majority of your time on a daily basis. Here are a few examples of some values:

1. Love
2. Creativity
3. Wealth
4. Health
5. Freedom
6. Fun
7. Happiness
8. Success
9. Learning/Education
10. Peace
11. Adventure
12. Friendship

This is just a small sampling of values, so please add others of your own preference. When you have a list of your current values, then prioritize these in the order you believe mean the most to you. The first 3 on your list will be where you'll focus a majority of your daily life. Keep this in mind when creating your list and your vision statement. You may find that your old values prior to your grief and loss are very different than your current values. When you determine what you desire in life and you gain clarity around how you'll move forward in your life, then you'll see that you'll begin to move out of the pain into pleasure. You'll no longer be "stuck" in that vicious cycle of pain without a clue how to heal and move forward.

It's very important to be congruent with your life and your values. If you're not congruent then you'll find that you won't find the happiness and peace you're looking for and you may sabotage your success. Therefore, when creating your roadmap to wholeness, it's important to be honest with yourself about exactly what's important to YOU now. This doesn't mean what's important to your spouse, your kids, your family or your career. This is for you to move towards a happier life filled with all your desires and your dreams. Moving through your grief is also a releasing process, so you must release all those things in your life that no longer serve you in the present life. It's a self-discovery process which will heal your mind, body and spirit by going to your heart and asking yourself what is it that YOU love? What kind of life do YOU want? Only YOU can answer those questions.

You'll want to take these exercises very seriously as if your life depended on it because it does. All of us only have a limited time in our physical existence here on Earth, so living your best life now is your pathway to happiness. By shining your light brightly, you give others permission to do the same. You can be happy again and live a life of your dreams with conscious choices you make on a daily basis, one day at a time. Avoid living in the past and the future; instead live in the present moment, for that's all you really have control over in your life. That being said, I want you to focus now in this moment and feel alive, take a breath in and let it out. You're alive and that's something to get excited about.

The Road Map To Be, Do, And Have

Now that you've established your values and created your personal vision statement, you now know your destination or as I like to refer to it your destiny. You also know where you are, don't you? There may be a big gap in where you are now compared to your destination. How do you get there? There are many ways to get there, but I'd like you to explore the map to be, do, and have.

BE – Who are you committed to being?

You'll have to ask yourself who you will have to be to accomplish your personal vision. There are certain ways of being that will catapult you moving forward toward your vision. I've found that the best way to do this is to make a list of people whom you admire and respect. Who are they being? Are they doing and having the things you most want in your personal vision? Make a list of qualities about yourself that you're committed to being and that will get you closer to your vision.

DO – What are you committed to doing?

This is another exercise for you to get complete clarity about the things you're doing on a daily basis to lead you to your personal vision statement. Make a list of all things that you must do to achieve your dream. You can mind map this if that helps you. What is a mind map? You can visit my website and download information on how to construct a mind map. I'll explain the process very briefly. You'll draw a circle and inside that circle, write one detail about your life, ie, finances, relationship, career, etc. Then draw several lines radiating from the circle outward like branches from a tree. On each branch, you'll write one idea that will result in your reaching your vision for that particular life area. Create as many branches as you can until you've run out of ideas. Then you'll begin incorporating each idea into your daily life one at a time, until you have achieved your vision and destination.

HAVE – WHAT ARE YOU COMMITTED TO HAVING?

In this exercise, you'll list all those things you want to have in your lifetime or that relate to your personal vision statement. What do you want to have when you reach your final destination? This doesn't have to be material possessions as it could be things you want to have such as a love relationship, a career you love, a legacy, peace of mind or living a life of joy. Although, you may want a new home, a new car or something that's of the material world.

CREATING YOUR ROADMAP TO WHOLENESS IN 90 DAYS

Congratulations on your journey so far on the road to wholeness. It takes courage and determination to make changes in your life. Once you've determined the "what" it is you're moving forward to achieve on the road to wholeness then you must determine the "how". So, I would like for you to begin incorporating all of the tools and techniques into your daily calendar to arrive at your final destination or personal vision statement.

You can do this! You may or may not reach your final destination or personal vision statement completely in 90 days, but you'll be well on your way to changing your life for the better and becoming a much happier person. You must move forward before you'll see the changes around you. More opportunities will be presented and revealed to you as you move forward with these new daily habits. You must have single mindedness of purpose and commitment to your personal vision.

Your mission, if you choose to accept it, is to plan your calendar daily to include all of the suggestions and exercises in this book, so you have a list of all the "soul"utions for healing your mind, body and spirit scheduled into your calendar. This will help you to remember your "soul"utions every day and get into the habit of self-love and self-care moving you forward towards wholeness. At first, you'll find that you'll have to think about each process, but after the first 30 days, you'll do most of these automatically as a part of your day because you'll find happiness and deep peace as a result. Once you're in the habit, you'll find that you can't miss a day without these "soul"utions because you feel so much better when you do them.

Here's an example of what your daily entry might look like:

1. Wake up after a restful sleep and start with Affirmative Prayer and Meditation.

2. Chakra Meditations using Affirmations for Healing.

3. Eat a healthy, organic breakfast in alignment with the season.

4. Walk, yoga, or other exercise.

5. Write in your gratitude journal every day listing at least 5 things you're grateful for.

6. Write in your journal about thoughts, intuition, dreams, desires and ideas.

7. Creative visualization exercise for your personal vision statement.

8. Incorporate the 5 Elements to balance your physical, emotional, mental and spiritual imbalances.

9. Incorporate "tools" for the spirit.

10. List at least 1 action step from your mind map to reach your personal vision statement.

Optional things to include:

1. Forgiveness Process.

2. Acceptance and Surrender Affirmative prayer.

3. Feng Shui for grief and loss.

4. All other processes you've found helpful.

As you incorporate these "soul"utions into your everyday life, you'll begin to notice a change in your awareness, your consciousness and the way you live your life. You won't be so easily affected by your external world, because you'll become very strong and happy with your internal world. As you begin to change your internal world, your external world will shift as well and you'll begin to attract all of those things that are in your personal vision statement.

In healing my emotional pain of grief and loss, I've utilized all of these healing "soul"utions in my quest for happiness, deep peace, love and joy. These have become a way of life for me, and I incorporate all of these processes into my daily life. Occasionally, I'll miss a day or sometimes a week if I'm traveling, and I begin to notice the imbalance with too much outer world and not enough inner world. I want you to know that I'm not only writing this book from the theoretical standpoint of all these concepts and principles, but I've utilized these tools myself with much success. I recommend this information to my coaching clients, and those who utilize this information seem to heal their emotional pain quicker and easier than those who don't use them. I didn't want to take antidepressants or any type of prescription drugs to make myself happy. I have the belief that if I'm in a state of emotional pain or discontent then the problem must be addressed at the cause so the desired effects in life will begin to show up. Drugs and alcohol only mask the pain, but don't address the cause. I made a personal decision that I wanted to be happy because I was sick and tired of being in pain, and I was going to do it holistically. So, I want you to know that by following the information given to you by God through me, you'll find that you will unlock the grief code within your mind, body and spirit. You'll find your way to living the life of your dreams, and I congratulate you!

Reaching Your Road To Wholeness Through Dream Analysis

A dream which is not understood

is like a letter that is not opened......Talmud

Every great journey begins with a dream. It's also said that dreams are the window to the soul. We spend half of our lives sleeping. I want to share with you a process that I've found to be truly helpful in doing my own dream analysis. Here's the step-by-step process:

1. Have a journal or notepad right next to your bed with a pen or pencil, and immediately upon awakening from your sleep, write down your dream. If you wait to do it later, you'll forget some of the details, so do it immediately upon awakening.

2. You'll take the dream and dissect it into symbols, patterns and literal translations.

3. Write down the meaning of those symbols and patterns.

4. Choose the context of life for which you're seeking answers, direction or guidance. It will usually be an issue or question you're currently dealing with during your day when you're awake. The context of life is your relationships, marriage, career, money, etc.

5. Determine the overall meaning of the dream. You are the only one who can interpret the symbols and patterns.

6. Action Step: Look at the messages and take action.

Dream Analysis Example #1: Context of life is Health

Symbol	_Meaning_	_Contextual Meaning_
Tropical Blue Water	Cleansing Emotions	Feeling Healthy

White Sand Beach	Comfortable/ Soothing	Content
Creatures jumping out of the water	Showing themselves creatively	Finding ways to create

Overall Meaning: When I feel healthy, I'm content. I need to find more creative ways of being healthy.

Action Steps: Enroll in a Salsa Dancing class and create foods that are healthy and delicious.

You'll find with practice that this will become easier and more fulfilling than you can imagine. We have unresolved issues in our unconscious mind that can be resolved with doing this dream analysis work. Also, you can set an intention to solve a problem or ask for guidance or direction with any life matter. Remember that nothing has any meaning except the meaning that you give it. That's why you must dissect and determine the symbols that are presented to you in your dreams.

Dream Analysis Example #2

The Dream

I went to unlock a car with a key. The car was parked along the curb of the road along with other cars. As I opened up the lock with the key, the car automatically turned on and rolled back and crashed into another car. There was a lot of damage done to the cars. People came out of their homes to see what had happened including the owner of the car, a man and his son. I walked away towards the end of the street and didn't look back. I got in my car and went home.

Symbols

Car – Movement

Key – The missing piece

Parked Car – Stagnation

Curb of the road – Temporary position

Other Cars – Other movement

Opened the lock with the key – finding the right piece

Car turns on automatically – It's a go!

Car rolls back and crashes into another car – Minor setback

Damage to the Cars – Hurts the movement forward

People – Not alone

Owner of the car and his son – Chief and son

Walked away – Left the scene

Got in my car – New movement forward

Interpretation

There's movement after finding the right missing piece, then stagnation occurs sidetracked by a temporary situation. There's other movement around me and help, and I found the right piece to move forward again. A minor setback hurts the movement forward. I'm not alone; there are other people to help. Leaving the minor setback, and then there's new movement forward.

Action Steps: No more procrastinating or temporary setbacks (self-sabotaging). I'm moving forward fearlessly regardless of obstacles in my path with the help of others. Let others help me find the right missing piece to help me in my new movement forward on my path.

As you can see from this example, you must dissect the symbols from the dream first and what these mean to you or literally what the symbols represent. You're the only one who can interpret your dream symbols, patterns and words. After you've listed the dream, the symbols and the interpretation, then you can see what action step is to be taken as a result of the dream. Enjoy the process!

This concludes the chapter on your roadmap to wholeness. I hope you'll implement all of the suggestions discussed in this chapter so you'll find the pathway to the peaceful heart and a renewed sense of love and joy in your life.

In the next chapter, you'll learn about purpose, passion and pleasure. Once you've laid the foundation for the roadmap to your personal vision statement, you'll then find your purpose, your passion for life and pleasure as a result. So, let's explore these in the next chapter.

Chapter 9

Your Purpose, Passion & Pleasure Map

*"The present moment is filled with joy and happiness.
If you are attentive, you will see it."*

—*Thich Nhat Hanh*

YOU'RE A VERY UNIQUE INDIVIDUAL with your own unique DNA footprint. Your DNA plays an important role in who you are, how you approach life and what roles you play in life. At the time of your birth, your DNA map is set and you come into the world with your unique footprint and life purpose. This is something that nobody else can do but you. It was what you were born to do. This DNA determines your life path based on your internal and external world. At the time you were born, there was energy present known as "Chi" at the exact time, day, month, year and place of your birth. This "Chi" is comprised of the 5 Elements: Wood, Fire, Earth, Metal and Water. This "Chi" that is connected with your DNA sets a certain energy pattern in motion in the form of the 5 elements that determines your strengths, weaknesses and life purpose. Of course, we always have choice in making decisions about our life, but often times, we don't know what our purpose in life is after experiencing grief and loss. We may have been living a life that was comfortable, and now things are changed and we don't really know where our life path is leading us. It's helpful to have such a tool to help you decide what your path is that will make you the happiest. The interaction of all the 5 Elements influences your life purpose map or your journey through time. The study of this is known as BaZi, the study of your destiny.

In chapter 6, on Healing the Physical Body, I explained the 5 Elements in relation to Traditional Chinese Medicine and how using the 5 Elements can assist in your healing of the physical body. In observing the 5 Elements, "Chi" flows within your birth chart; it will also indicate your best path leading to happiness and overall well-being based on your core strengths. This is about empowering yourself to make the most of what life has to offer now that you're entering a new beginning in your life after loss. This will allow you to make better informed life and business decisions, maximize your true potential, strengthen relationships in your personal and professional life, understand other people in your life and business and choose the right career path for you and your life purpose. When you're not sure about what to do and where you're going next, it's helpful to look into your BaZi chart to determine some choices for you. This is a very complex discipline that requires years of extensive training to analyze a BaZi chart. I would like you to know that this is available to you with my grief recovery coaching programs. Together, we'll review the most empowering life path for you in your journey to wholeness. You'll begin to notice that you have choices that will feed your soul and put you in direct alignment with your life purpose and your path to happiness. You'll welcome this opportunity to know more about yourself to be able to design your destiny knowing that you're utilizing your greatest strengths, skills and talents. Then you'll be using these strengths, skills and talents given to you by the Divine so that you could live a life of your dreams on purpose with passion and enjoying every moment of every day in love with life.

MORE ON LIFE PURPOSE AND PASSION

There are some additional questions that will help guide you on your way to your life purpose and your passion. Of course, the BaZi analysis is the most profound tool that I've found in my journey for self-realization. I've been studying and doing BaZi charts for over a decade, and it's served me and my clients well. However, here are some questions that you can ask yourself to begin to notice your purpose and passions in life. These questions will get you started on your path to awareness of your gifts, talents and passions.

1. What and who did you want to become when you were a child? What activities did you love to do when you were a child? Make a list or write a paragraph about you as a child. What did you find?

2. What did you do well in life or find complete joy in doing? Where do you get lost in an activity and lose track of time because you're having so much fun?

3. What would you say are your greatest talents and natural abilities?

4. What would others say are your greatest talents and natural abilities? You could ask your closest friends or family members this question.

5. What are you really passionate about?

6. If money or time wasn't a factor, what would you spend your time doing?

7. Is there one question that you've asked all your life or one question that's driven your behavior all your life?

8. What would you like to contribute to the world?

9. In reviewing the answers to all the above questions, how do you think these answers are related to your life purpose and your passion in life?

After you answer these questions for yourself, you'll begin to notice that the answers may give you an indication of your life purpose or passions in life. Often times when you look at your childhood past times, your greatest achievements, your hobbies or where you spend your free time is where you'll find the answers to your life purpose and passion for life. If you have a glimpse of what that may be then you're on the road to success.

Since we just finished a chapter on our core values and the personal vision statement, how does our life purpose and passion affect the whole? These should all be congruent with each other so you're in alignment with your core values while you're on the road to your personal vision statement and you're living your life with passion and on purpose. This, my friends, is the formula for a happy life. So, you have some work to do now, don't you? Please put the time into these self-realization exercises and you'll find many rewards. You don't want to live your life by default as the majority of the population does, making decisions based on their external circumstances. No, this is backwards! You make your decisions about YOU, and then you live your life congruent with your core values, your personal vision statement, your life purpose and your passion for life. This is the universal law of manifesting your desires into form so they begin to show up in your life in the external world, and you've created a life of your dreams.

Pleasure

I want to include the topic of pleasure in this chapter, because I believe it's a forgotten principle in our culture but very necessary to lead a completely happy life. How many times were you told as a child to "get all your work done first" so you could then experience pleasure and go play? As we grow up into adulthood and we have increased responsibilities in life, we forget that pleasure is a part of life. There's something inside ourselves that says pleasure needs to be earned or that we're not worthy to have pleasure in our life. Especially after experiencing grief or loss, we may feel that we don't deserve to be happy or have pleasure in our life. I remember having these thoughts after my husband died. I didn't deserve to have pleasure in my life without him. I couldn't express pleasure or happiness in my life, because then I would not be honoring my deceased husband. I felt guilty for enjoying myself and seeking pleasure, but in reality that was the key to my healing the grief and loss. So, please don't deny yourself pleasure in your life after grief and loss. You deserve to have pleasure in life.

The Gateway To Happiness Is Pleasure

The opposite of pleasure is pain, and the gateway to happiness is pleasure. You're now going from your pain to pleasure, so congratulate yourself for having the courage to drop all those old limiting beliefs and move forward in life incorporating some type of pleasure into your life.

It's important to understand and create a map for pleasure. When we leave this world and transition into the next, it's been said that one of the life review questions that's asked is, "Did you experience pleasure?" Then the next question is, "What kind of pleasure did you experience?"

The more evolved our soul becomes and developed as we become a person, the more conscious we become of incorporating pleasure into our lives, and the level of depth of pleasure and happiness seems to increase. However, we must understand that there must be discernment in pleasures, rules for pleasure and levels of pleasure.

Addictions can be termed a pleasure, but we know that this isn't healthy pleasure. There's no balance in a pleasure such as an addiction. It's a pleasure that's only achieved when there's a dopamine fix when only a certain kind of event takes place. Eventually, all other pleasures don't give you pleasure and the pleasure becomes a survival mechanism. There's a collapse and a destruction of the ability to have pleasures. It's at this point that pleasure must be relearned. So, I'm not talking here about the pleasures that are related to addictions. Addictions are being attracted to what you're missing, and remember as a whole person, you're not missing anything. I'm talking about balanced pleasure that keeps us healthy, adds to our life and makes us very happy in our journey through life.

There are some rules for having pleasure that I would like to mention.

1. Pleasure is a skill that needs to be developed for most people. There's an art form to gaining the skill of pleasure.

2. There is pain, comfort and pleasure. The opposite of pleasure is pain. By releasing the pain and moving towards pleasure, you must give up a level of comfort to have authentic pleasure.

3. Mature pleasure is based on delayed gratification.

4. The deeper and more refined the pleasure, the longer it takes to learn. The greater the pleasure, the more skill or effort it takes to learn.

5. Every pleasure has its price.

6. Every pleasure has its spiritual practice.

7. You must enjoy the pleasure and then let it go. The refusal to let it go is an addiction.

When you're contemplating adding a pleasure to your life, please take into consideration the rules for pleasure. There are also levels of pleasure.

1. **Level 1** – This level includes all forms of physical pleasures using the 5 senses and the pleasures that they give. This one doesn't require much skill or effort and it doesn't require delayed gratification, ie, fast food, comfort, quick fixes. These can be exchanged for other pleasures in levels 2 to 6, especially at the higher level of consciousness.

2. **Level 2** – This is the pleasure of love, affection and relationships.

It takes skill and effort, and there's no rate of exchange for this pleasure.

3. **Level 3** – Ideals and being aligned with a cause. This takes practice, effort and time, and there's no rate of exchange for this pleasure. Identify a cause you're willing to die for and live for it.

4. **Level 4** – Pleasure of enlightenment. This is where you shift from the separate self to Oneness of all there is in the Universe. There's no rate of exchange for this one.

5. **Level 5** – Unique self-image and creativity. You're the artist of your own destiny and you must create at all costs. You're living your unique story or your soul purpose. There's no rate of exchange for this one.

6. **Level 6** – Unique obligation pleasure that aligns you with the Universe. This is identified with a real need that you recognize and it can only be met by you alone.

When you look at the levels of pleasure, you can understand that as we increase levels the pleasure becomes more profound and is of a higher evolution. Level 1 being all the physical pleasures are easily substituted, so you want to incorporate the higher levels of pleasure into your life for true happiness. I believe all of you reading my book can attain a level 5 pleasure by living your core values, achieving your personal vision statement and living your unique purpose with passion and pleasure. That's my wish for all of you.

Chapter 10

The Tao Of Healing Using Feng Shui Principles For Grief And Loss

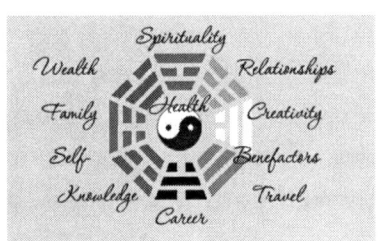

"Thirty spokes converge upon a single hub; It is on the hole in the center that the use of the cart hinges. We make a vessel from a lump of clay: It is the empty space within the vessel that makes it useful. We make doors and windows for a room; But it is these empty spaces that make the room liveable. Thus, while the tangible has advantages, it is the intangible that makes it useful."

—Tao The Ching

Introduction to Feng Shui

This book, Healing the Mind, body and spirit from grief and loss, would not be complete unless the following chapter is included in addressing the environment in which we live and work. In the preceding chapters, the internal world has been viewed from a holistic perspective of healing the body, mind and spirit. Now we will take a look at healing the external world for the person who is in grief or has experienced a loss. The environments in which we live, work and play either create a healthy existence or one of "dis-ease". Therefore, it is so important to create a nurturing, abundant environment especially after experiencing grief and loss that will feed you on every level of your existence: mental, emotional, physical and spiritual

You can create this by implementing the ancient Chinese Art and Science of Feng Shui within your environment and these principles have been utilized for over 4,000 years. Feng Shui is one of the 8 rays of Traditional Chinese Medicine. It is the study of heaven and earth in relation to humans and all living things. The Chinese referred to this as the "San Cai" or the Three Gifts. It is the meeting of the visible, invisible and the vibrational worlds together to achieve harmony and balance in an environment.

Feng Shui, pronounced "fung shway," literally translated means "wind and water". Wind and water are the two forces that are the carrier of "Chi" or energy that exist in movement and contain life force. This "Chi" is contained in all things that exist in the physical world. This energy is constantly moving and changing to achieve balance and harmony. When using Feng Shui for healing, we desire containment of the "Chi" energy to be grounded, directed and held in a specific manner so to achieve the greatest harmony and balance. It is the visible and invisible energy patterns or "Chi" within a home, office or landscape that effects the environment where we live and work. This "Chi" affects us energetically on all levels of our existence. If we are not living in homes or working in offices that are in harmony and nurture us then on an energetic level it is affecting every aspect of the physical, emotional, mental and spiritual levels of our world.

Everything is energy that exists in the physical world. When our environment affects our internal energy systems in a negative way this results in resistance. The negative impact or resistance may lead to disease, death, divorce, financial crisis, discordant relationships, and more. By applying the correct Feng Shui principles, you can achieve harmony and balance within your environment leading you to heal from the heartbreak of grief and loss.

Feng Shui is sometimes referred to as ***"acupuncture for the home"***. As a practitioner of acupuncture or acupressure would diagnose the blocked energy pathways within the meridians of the human body and try to unblock these pathways with certain pressure points or needles, so a Feng Shui Practitioner looks for blockages within the pathways of the home or environment. These specific points are targeted with Feng Shui adjustments and/or cures and the blocked area changes its energy patterns and a shift occurs in that space. That explains why when you move your furniture around in a room it takes on an entirely different feel as well as the appearance because the energy has shifted. We invite in and accelerate change in our lives. This happens when we move to a new home, add on to the existing home or build a new home. We are changing the flow of the energy patterns and opening up blocked areas, increasing the flow and circulation and this changes everything.

Feng Shui and the Elemental You

You may know a little, or a lot, about Feng Shui already. It is my intention to share with you some insights about Feng Shui and the Five Elements that you may not know and how these elements affect you, your environment and your destiny. Are you interested? If you are, then you are in the right place, at the right time, to effect change in your life. There are three key elements that affect you, your environment, and your destiny. Let's move ahead to review these three key elements.

Your Heaven Luck

The first one is known as "Heaven Luck." This affects you as a person based on the cosmology of the Universe. This is known as Chinese Astrology, BaZi or the Four Pillars of Destiny. This is the study of the stars, planets and astrological energy flows that are in the Universe, and the elements that make up you, as a person. These can be a combination of Fire, Earth, Metal, Water and Wood in addition to the 12 Chinese animals. This method determines your soul's path, strengths, weaknesses, and what energy flows and cycles you are currently encountering in your life. Do you think that this may have an impact on your current life situation? Absolutely it does. It is very important during a Feng Shui consultation to analyze the current life cycle of an individual and their elemental make-up to determine remedies for the environment and to assist in the decisions of future endeavors and current life situations.

Your Earth Luck

The second factor is your "Earth Luck," known as the Feng Shui of your environment. This is the method that you probably know a little or a lot about from the reading of many books on the subject of Feng Shui. However, did you know that there are actually three main methodologies that are used in Feng Shui to analyze a home, office or landscape? Most Practitioners specialize in one methodology or they may use a combination of these. These three different methods are known as: **Black Hat Tantric Buddism or BTB**, **Classical Feng Shui**, and *Form School*.

The **Black Hat Tantric Buddism or BTB** method is the method based on the front door and how the Bagua compass (which I will discuss in detail next) aligns over the floor plan or landscape based on the Lo Shu Magic Square (shown below). This is the most recognized method from which most books are written about in today's western world.

The **Classical or Taoist Feng Shui** method is based on directions, energy flow patterns within the space and time analysis using the Lo Pan Compass. This method also takes into consideration the birth information of the occupants when making a Feng Shui analysis.

The third method is used in conjunction with both the Black Hat and Classical Feng Shui methods. It is known as **Form School**, and this method is based on land forms which are beneficial to the building and its location on the land and surrounding influences of the local geographic area. The principles are also used inside the dwelling for nurturing energy flows within the space, based on nature.

All three methods have proven to be effective for creating abundant environments with thriving lives that create positive change and influence for the occupants.

Your Human Luck

The third level is "Human Luck." The Human Luck consists of the choices that we make in life and how this affects us on all levels of our physical, emotional, mental and spiritual life. If the "Heaven Luck" appears to be favorable within the person's birth chart and the "Earth Luck" indicates favorable Feng Shui influences; however results in life are unfavorable, then we must review the Human Luck. This is where the healing of the mind is relevant. Are you running those old programs of the mind that are no longer serving you? Are you in a hypnotic state of disempowerment? Do you lack motivation and self-confidence to live the life of your dreams? These old mind programs will surely affect the Feng Shui of your environment and the elemental you in moving forward to achieve all of your desires and dreams. This is a key factor that cannot be ignored when addressing grief and loss. However, by making some positive shifts in life choices, everything can change for the better. When the "Human Luck" is combined with the "Heaven and Earth Luck" amazing miracles can happen in transforming your grief to happiness.

Did you think Feng Shui was just about hanging a crystal or moving your couch? Well, I hope I have given you some insights into the total world of Feng Shui and how it can help you to affect change, prosperity and abundance in your life.

The Bagua Compass

The Bagua Compass or Map used in Feng Shui is made up of the 8 Trigrams of the I-Ching. The I-Ching is an ancient text that is known as The Book Of Changes. This may be the oldest book known in existence and it contains ancient wisdom and great insights. How did this come about? It all began with the Emperor and the Tortoise. The legend has it that Fu His, a great Emperor, sat meditating on the banks of the Yangtze River when a tortoise appeared to him from out of the water's edge. This great Emperor was in a great state of meditation and saw upon the tortoise shell the markings and the pattern of the Lo-Shu Magic Square. This is a unique mathematical structure arranged in 3 columns of numbers 1 through 9 that add up to fifteen in any direction. The Lo-Shu Magic Square was used to identify patterns for Chinese numerology, astrology, and Feng Shui

The Lo-Shu Magic Square

4	9	2
3	5	7
8	1	6

The numbers of the Lo-Shu Magic Square were translated by the great emperor into the 8 Trigrams of the I-Ching or also known as The Book Of Changes. These later were translated into the Bagua compass or Map. These 8 Trigrams each represent a different aspect of a person's life and are placed within the home, office or landscape and serve as the energy template within that space for that life experience. These are labeled as the following:

1 = Career or Life Path = North

2 = Marriage or Relationships = Southwest

3 = Family or Ancestors = East

4 = Wealth, Prosperity & Abundance = Southeast

5 = Health and Tai Chi = Middle

6 = Benefactors, Helpful People and Travel = Northwest

7 = Children and Creativity = West

8 = Self-Cultivation and Wisdom = Northeast

9 = Fame, Reputation and Spirituality = South

We use these directions and life areas to align within our environment whether it be our home, office or landscape. We can access and transform the energetic invisible and visible energy patterns in our material world with Feng Shui. In addition, Feng Shui works with our environment to help achieve harmony and balance as a reflection and mirror for our internal world. Our environment tells us and the world who we are and we can use this to change ourselves by changing our environment. Our energy and that of our environment is constantly changing. Our level of consciousness about our environment reflects our inner self in our surroundings consciously or unconsciously. The places in our home where we spend the most time affect us the most and it is most important to know the energy patterns you are surrounding yourself with when you are healing from grief or loss. So, now let us look at each area in detail, so you can begin to make changes in your environment for greater harmony and balance.

The Pathway To Healing Using The Bagua

You will use the Bagua Blueprint to align with the interior floor plan of the home, office or landscape. I will begin with the 8 life sectors, including the middle sector, and describe the attributes and characteristics for each area so you can begin to determine where you want to apply Feng Shui in your home or office. When you align and correlate the Bagua Blueprint with your floor plan, you will begin to notice where the necessary changes must be made to clear the "stuck" energy patterns to allow for harmony and balance in the flow of that particular life sector. You will begin to release aspects of your life that are no longer serving you to allow room for the new to unfold in your life.

I would like to say that this is just basic Feng Shui guidance using the Classical Feng Shui method. I am not including any information on the Black Hat Tantric Buddism method or Form School method in this book. I prefer using the Classical Feng Shui method in my work and that is why I have used it here as a guide for you to use. A complete Feng Shui consultation would be much more complex than what is given in this chapter on healing grief and loss with Feng Shui. This is to introduce you to Feng Shui concepts and the ways you can begin incorporating Feng Shui into your environment to begin healing the external environment which will lead to a shift internally on all levels of mind, body and spirit. If you would like more information about a complete Feng Shui consultation then please go to my website.

So, let's begin with Sectors 1 – 9 of the Bagua Blueprint with Basic Feng Shui principles:

Sector 1- Career or Life Path Area – North

This sector is located in the North of the home or office and is the area that correlates with your career, life path, job, hobbies, interests, opportunities, volunteer work or other individualized skills. Its energy element is water. The colors associated with this area are blue, black, or colors of water. This area carries the energy of water and the ability to go with the flow of life like water. It is important to connect with spirit and dive deep in to spiritual practices with trust and faith that we are being guided along our journey and to be open to new opportunities that come into our life. Like water, the shape associated with this area are curved and waved objects that represent water-like qualities. The body parts associated with this area are the ears and kidneys. If you are experiencing difficulty hearing your guidance, then this is the place to look for "stuck" energy patterns in relation to your career or life path. Also, the kidneys represent filtering and allowing absorption of water in the body. So by releasing what no longer serves you and allowing the new flow to enter your life, you will balance this life sector. Add the colors of water to this area including water features and water influences to enhance the flow. These are often recommended for this area unless there is a problem placing water in the North based on the yearly energy influences. You can always visit my website at www.sandraruggles.com for more information about the yearly water influences.

Sector 2 – Marriage and Relationship Area – Southwest

This sector is located in the Southwest of the home or office and is the area that correlates with marriage and relationships that are loving and nurturing. The colors associated with this area are red, pink and white. These colors should be incorporated in to this area to enhance the energy for this life sector. This area carries the energy of earth and the shape consists of a square. This is an excellent area to place wedding pictures, pictures of loved ones, paired items, crystals, plants, and pottery in the colors for the area. The body parts are the stomach and female organs of the body. This is where you receive nourishment for love, fertility, romance and marriage. If you are seeking a new relationship, then this is the area you will want to work with to enhance the energy flows for a new partner to arrive. This is where we open to the goodness of what life has to bring us next after grief or loss. It is important to love yourself first before you can open your heart to another. We must be consciously aware of our needs and to be centered within ourselves in order to "call in" a satisfying relationship. I highly recommend the book, "Calling

In The One", by Katherine Woodward Thomas. Read this book while working on your Feng Shui and you will see huge results. For more information on group classes in person and on-line, please visit my website www.sandraruggles.com.

Sector 3 - Family and Ancestors – East

This sector is located in the East of the home or office and is the area that correlates with your family and ancestors. The color for this area is green and the element is wood. The shape for this area is rectangular items and the body part is the feet. The family does not need to be of origin but could be a family of choice such as: congregations, religious and spiritual affiliations. It includes the animal kingdom family as well. This area is great for a family room or dining area where the family of the house will congregate. Whatever room falls in the East would be considered the family and ancestors area. This is a great area to display family photos and family traditions. The family legacy and ancestral symbols belong here. The wood energy symbolizes our "roots" and like a tree is always growing and getting stronger so should the relationship with family and the ancestors. You should place items here that represent your foundation and core beliefs so that these become the symbols for your growth within the home and family.

Sector 4 – Wealth, Prosperity and Abundance – Southeast

This sector is located in the Southeast area of the home or office and is considered the wealth, prosperity and abundance area. The colors for this area are purple, red, blue, black and green. There are many colors to incorporate into this area. The element is small wood representing plants and the shape is rectangular. This area is represented by hips, legs and bones. This area is about giving and receiving wealth, prosperity and abundance within the universal flow. Some of the items you may place here would include: money tokens, piggy banks, affirmations for prosperity, money cures, and other relevant symbols for abundance and prosperity based on what that means for you. It doesn't have to be related to money because wealth, abundance and prosperity comes in many forms and this is very individualized based on the occupants. You may place powerful affirmations and symbols representing all that feeds your soul. You may ask yourself the question, "What is abundance to me?" Then you will place those pictures or symbols in the area to remind yourself of these things and incorporate these in your life. It is important that this area remains clutter free so there is no "stuck" energy patterns that will block your wealth, prosperity and abundance. What does this area say to you energetically? Do you feel powerful or abundant in the space? You will know if you need to change things here after answering the above questions. When you clean up your wealth corner, it will allow for more abundance and prosperity to enter into your life.

Sector 5 – Health and the Tai Chi – Center of the Home or Office

This sector is located in the center of the home or office and is considered the health or overall well-being area. It is referred to as the Tai Chi of the dwelling. It is the Chinese belief that when all the other sectors of the home or office are in balance, so is the health and overall well-being of the occupants. This is so important when you are overcoming grief and loss to have your entire life in balance. This area usually consists of a hallway, but it could be a room depending on the floor plan. The colors associated with this area are earth tones, yellow, and gold. The element is earth and the shape is square. The body parts are all the other body parts not mentioned in all other areas. It is used for all health intentions and should be symbolized as such with earth type objects such as pottery, crystals, and stones. This area is great for vibrant photos representing good health, affirmations for healing and symbols for balance in all life areas.

Sector 6 – Benefactors, Helpful People or Travel – Northwest

This sector is located in the Northwest corner of the home or office. It contains the energy of people coming into your life to help you achieve your desires and dreams. It is the helpful people in your life that create our greatest support systems to move forward achieving goals and tasks that are important to us. This is the area where we connect with other celestial beings, ascended masters and our guides. This is the area to pray to your deities to make contact with spirit and be open to receiving guidance and assistance. This area also carries the energy for travel. When we travel, we are expanding our horizons and learning new ideas and experiences which lead to new beginnings and an expansion of consciousness. The colors for this area are grey, white and black. The element for this area is metal and the shape is round. So include these in this area to enhance the space. This is a great place to set up an altar or sacred space for prayer and meditation. The body part associated with this area is the head which relates to the sixth and seventh chakras of the third eye and the crown chakra. This area is where intuition is exemplified with prayer and meditation allowing the divine flow from the Universe. The northwest corner is excellent for a meditation room. Place objects here that will allow your higher self to be open and receptive to higher wisdom and knowledge.

Sector 7 – Children and Creativity – West

This sector is located in the West area of the home or office. It contains the energy for children and creativity of the occupants. This is the area of play and the creative arts such as painting, writing, playing music or any creative endeavors of the heart. The colors for this area are white, pastels and metallic. The element is metal and the shape is round. The body part associated with this area is the mouth. So speaking our truth and finding our voice is very important in how we communicate with the world. Expressing our creativity and our inner child is essential to growing in our own evolution after grief and loss. This area makes a wonderful children's play room or a space to express your creative arts. You may display your artwork here or place symbols for music, writing, and inspiration for your creativity. Use metal and round objects here in the space to exemplify the energy and expand your awareness in the creative essence of your soul.

Sector 8 – Self-Cultivation, Knowledge or Wisdom – Northeast

This sector is located in the Northeast area of the home or office. This area represents the sector of deep thinking, growth and wisdom. The colors for this area are blue, green and black. The element is Earth and the shape is square. The body part associated with this area is the hands. This is a very powerful area in the home for spiritual growth and healing. It makes a wonderful meditation room, den or library specifically for academic work. This is a great place to store books on bookshelves that relate to inspiration and self-cultivation. Pictures and symbols representing inspiration and learning are good to place in this area. It is important to explore your inner world here and go deep to gain a greater understanding of who you are and how to get in touch with your basic nature on a soul level. At this point, you connect with spirit and open up to receiving all the universal truths leading to greater wisdom and self-cultivation. Place symbols and objects here that are in the colors of the area and represent your cultivation and growth.

Sector 9 – Fame, Reputation and Spirituality – South

This sector is located in the South area of the home or office. The color for this area is red and the element is fire. Since fire is the element for the area, it is necessary to have good lighting that is not too dark so as to increase the fame and reputation in a positive manner. The shape is triangular and the body part is the eyes. The eyes are said to be the "window to the soul" which is our sense of self. When we decide to make changes in our lives and move forward, this is where we would place those pictures, symbols and objects representing our personal reputation and who you are becoming in the future. It is a good place to display achievements, awards, affirmations for growth and diplomas. It exemplifies the energy to get the word out to the world who you are and what you do. This is the area of illumination so place objects here that represent your fame, reputation and spirituality. This is another great place for an altar or sacred space because it carries the energy for the spirituality center.

Clear The Clutter – Heal The Mind, Body And Spirit

It is important to add this section on clearing clutter when you are trying to heal from grief or loss. It is so important to remove clutter from your environment when you are experiencing any transition in life. Where there is clutter there is stagnation or "stuck" energy and if you are "stuck" in your grief then removing clutter will help you to move the energy in your home and in yourself so you can move forward towards a healthier life. As within so without. So remove all clutter in your external world and watch your internal world shift as a result.

I have found working with many clients over the years that when there is significant clutter in their home or office, they often have a hard time finding the energy to begin to clear it out. This is the result of the stagnant Chi energy that you are connected to. It literally drains you of all your energy and exhaustion is the end result. So by releasing those things that no longer serve you or have significance in your life, you are releasing the "stuck" energy and allowing it to flow freely through your home and in your life. If you are experiencing fatigue and exhaustion in your life at the current time, then you must look at where your holding on to the damaging clutter influences in your home or office.

I have worked with clients who have a resistance to releasing personal possessions because they believe that someday they will "need" this or that item in their home or office. However, if you haven't used the item within one year, and it serves no purpose in your life, then it is time to let it go to someone who can use it or discard it. It keeps the energy flow moving so new items can come into your life that represent who you are at the present time. There is no purpose keeping those things in your life that you no longer use or enjoy. That includes gifts and presents from family or friends. It is very generous to receive and give a gift, but if you don't enjoy the gift or even like the gift, then it is time for it to be passed to another who can benefit from its use. By hanging on to possessions because we think someday this item will be needed, you are sending the message to the Universe that you are in lack of trust that the Universe will provide what you need always and forever. It is the scarcity mindset that says you must hang on to it because you may not be able to afford to replace it down the road. So that is exactly what the Universe will bring you, scarcity. You must know that the Universe will always provide what you need when you need it and have trust and faith that all your needs will be met. You do not need to "hang on" to anything that you no longer are using, that no longer serves you, or you desire in your home or office. Give yourself the permission to release and let go into the flow of abundance and prosperity!

5 Simple Steps To Clearing Clutter

1. I suggest viewing and analyzing your home or office by walking from room to room and making a priority list of the areas that you determine need decluttering. That will get you started identifying the areas that need your attention. You can assign each area a number based on priority to declutter. This will help you to get focused.

2. In your calendar, schedule a full day or even a couple of hours per week to begin going through the cluttered areas. You must set time in your schedule or you may never get to it. You can start with one drawer or one room at a time depending on how

much time you have or want to spend decluttering. Begin with the room or areas that you determine need it the most. If you are having problems with money, you may wish to start in the wealth, prosperity and abundance area of the home first.

3. While going through the clutter, it is best to stage it in an area where you can sort it into three separate piles which consist of:

    a. Organizing the items you are going to keep.

    b. Discarding the items that can be thrown away.

    c. Packing up the items that you want to give away or donate to your favorite charity.

4. Organize the items that you wish to keep in an area that is best suited for that item. Remember to only keep those things that you use and lift you up and nourish your soul.

5. Give yourself permission to let things go, so you can begin to allow room for the new to come into your life.

6. Celebrate your success when you complete each step in the clutter clearing process.

INTERIOR SPACE CLEARING

After you have completed clearing all the clutter from your home or office, then it is beneficial to perform interior space clearing before you put your Feng Shui design and cures in place. The space clearing allows for purification of the interior energies within the home or office. There are many reasons why an interior space clearing is performed and here is a list of some of the reasons why this is so important in a home or business when someone is overcoming grief and loss:

1. *Space Clearing for Healing* – When a space is cleared it promotes the healing on a physical, emotional, mental and spiritual level.

There is energy that accumulates in the space that is released by the emotions on an energetic level and when a space clearing is performed, the air is cleansed and purified with a renewed sense of healing in the space. I have had many clients that have suffered from grief, depression and anxiety problems which were healed when we did space clearing in their home. They reported feeling better within days.

2. ***Space Clearing for Predecessor Energy*** – Predecessor energy is energy that is residual and left over from prior occupants of a home or office. It is about the history of the home or business and who had been there before and what problems occurred in the home or business. This energy tends to stagnate and repeat itself unless it is cleared and removed. For example, if there was illness, death or divorce in a home then it is quite possible that the prior occupants had experienced the same difficulties due to the residual energy that is held in the space. So, it is wise to do a space clearing in the home to remove the old predecessor energy of the prior occupants, so the new occupants can move in with a completely fresh start. This will eliminate the possibility that future occupants will be affected by similar difficulties.

3. ***Space Clearing after a Death*** - It is necessary in the State of California for a real estate professional to disclose there was a death in a property that is being sold. When someone dies in a home due to an illness, suicide, or an accident, it is necessary to do a space clearing because of the negative effects of the discordant energy after death that reside in the home or office. This lingers in the space and must be purified to release it to return to peace and harmony within the energetic space of the home or business once again. I have cleared many residences where a murder or suicide took place and because of my sensitivity to energy, I could feel the heaviness of the trauma lingering through the space that had to be cleared before peace and harmony could be returned. This energy affects all the occupants on an energetic

level. This is so important after losing a loved one who died at home or one who had a long lingering illness. It is so refreshing to cleanse and purify the space so that the heaviness can be released and harmony restored.

4. *Space Clearing after an Illness* – It is necessary to cleanse a space after an illness to purify from germs and energetic residue that is remaining in a space. Doesn't it feel really great to wash your sheets and clean a room after you have been sick from the flu or a cold? In a hospital room or bedroom, it is very necessary to cleanse the space after someone has been ill for any period of time. It just washes away all the heaviness that seems to reside in the energy of the room, and creates a fresh, clean area for the next patient or occupant.

5. *Space Clearing for New Beginnings* – I love to do a space clearing when someone moves into a new home. It is great to start off with a clean slate purifying from the prior occupants if it is resale or from the construction if it is a new home. It is wise to do a new home blessing and clearing ceremony anytime you move into a new home, apartment or any new residence. It is also done for new businesses as well. Anytime a business changes owners or opens for the first day of business, it is wise to do a space clearing to welcome in the new and release the old.

6. *Space Clearing for Change* - A space clearing is done anytime you would like a shift in the energy of the space. This can sometimes be done at a New Moon, Full Moon, Winter/Summer Solstice, or the Fall/Spring Equinox. Any event that requires change or a shift will benefit from the purification ceremony. It can be done when the energy in a home or business just doesn't feel right, healthy or you would like something to change. Anytime you do a space clearing, it is like a spring cleaning of all that was there energetically to release it and replace with the new fresh beginning. You will see a big difference in the feeling of the space and your vitality after a space clearing for change.

There are many more reasons to do a space clearing or a purification ceremony, but these that are listed here are the ones most necessary after grief or loss. I hope you will consider incorporating this ancient ritual of space clearing into your life to allow free flowing energy throughout your home or business. Remember to do this after you have cleared the clutter and before your Feng Shui placement. You will see huge results in your Feng Shui placement when combined with clutter clearing and space clearing. Your life will shift as a result and you will then experience a new beginning to move forward in creating your dreams and desires.

How To Do A Space Clearing In Your Home Or Office

1. Thoroughly clean and declutter the space prior to space clearing.

2. Do the space clearing during the day when there is plenty of light.

3. Do not do a space clearing if you are pregnant, menstruating or sick.

4. Do a space clearing when you are feeling centered, mentally alert and physically healthy.

5. Take a shower or bath and be clean and well groomed when doing the space clearing.

6. Do a space clearing in silence without any background noise from music or television.

7. Pets are very sensitive to a space clearing so it is best to remove them from the space while doing the space clearing. They can feel the energetic shifts and it may be upsetting to them. It has been my experience that this is true for most dogs and cats.

8. Set up an area for all the space clearing tools so you will have everything you need.

9. You can burn sage, light candles, disperse essential oils, burn incense, or use holy water to purify the space as you walk from room to room.

10. Walk through the entire space with your scents listed above and say out loud a prayer, an affirmation, or a mantra as you walk from room to room releasing the scent and speaking loud and clear with clarity and intention to purify the space of all residual energy.

11. Invite the Divine Presence, Angels, Guides and Ascended Masters to assist with the purification of the space.

12. You can use bells, gongs, singing bowls, clapping your hands, or any type of sound that will disperse the energy in a room.

13. It is best if you do this alone, so you can focus your intention on clearing the energy.

14. Walk through the entire space with pure intention of purification, bringing in the light of the divine and removing any residual negative energy that may be lingering in the space.

15. You will know when you are done because you will feel the energetic shift.

16. Celebrate the shifts that occur as a result of your space clearing.

Congratulations on shifting the energy in your home or office! There are many mystical ancient methods of clearing energy in a home or office, but this one listed above is very simple and easy to use. I have specific videos on my website for space clearing techniques that I have learned over the years and used with my clients for significant results in clearing the energy of a space. Energy clearings can also be done for land parcels and landscapes. You can learn more by going to my website www.sandraruggles.com about space clearing techniques.

Color Therapy For Healing From Grief Or Loss

There are certain colors that align with the Feng Shui Bagua Compass or Map that were mentioned previously in this chapter. There are specific reasons why these colors are suggested for those particular sectors.

Color affects us on a cellular level and can affect our moods and our feelings. That is why it is important to be very conscious of the colors we choose for our décor and walls in our homes and offices. Each area of the Bagua Map has corresponding colors recommended and these create a vibrational frequency for that particular life sector. That vibrational frequency will affect your mind, body and spirit. It is very important that we choose colors for our environment that we love and feed our soul. Also, it is important that we choose colors that match the vibration of the activities and placement of the rooms as well. For example, a bright fire engine red color would not be a good choice for a bedroom because red is a very yang or active color that promotes action. In a bedroom, you do not want action or alertness when you are trying to get a restful sleep. Our bedrooms should be for rest and rejuvenation to heal the body while it is sleeping and a better color that resonates with that is the color blue or green. So, you must choose the right color vibration for the activity of the room, so you can achieve the balance and harmony of the space.

Here are some colors that are included in the Bagua Map and a description of what each color symbolizes. This information can be found in the book, "Living Color", Master Lin Yun's Guide to Feng Shui and the Art of Color by Sarah Rossbach and Lin Yun. This is a great book all about color and Feng Shui if you would like to know more. Additionally, I have added my own comments based on my experience with color and Feng Shui over the years working with it.

Red – The color red is considered very auspicious or "lucky" in Feng Shui. That is why in BTB Feng Shui we use red envelopes for wealth, prosperity and abundance. It ignites and stimulates feelings, conversations and activity. It promotes happiness, warmth and passion. It stimulates the brain and the skin. It encourages increased energy flow, excitement and strength.

Purple – The color purple or any variation of purple is another very auspicious color. It resonates with respect, nobility, fortune and power. It is a very spiritual color and resonates with the spirit because it holds so much richness. Royalty always wore the color purple and had purple in their environment because it was the color that was the most expensive to create. Therefore, it has always been associated with money, power and royalty.

Yellow – The color yellow produces maximum illumination and represents light. It also resonates with power, patience, tolerance, loyalty and wisdom. It is used in real estate as an exterior house paint color because it promotes a sense of comfort and security. Many homes that are painted the color yellow seem to sell quicker than others. So, yellow is a good choice if your considering selling your home.

Green – The color green is a very healing color and should be used in a healing environment. As you may notice, many hospitals and institutions use the color green. It also resonates to tranquility, growth, hope, awakening and freshness. It symbolizes the wood element in Feng Shui which consists of plants and gardens which are the color of green and growth.

Blue – The color blue is a great color for meditation and association with turning inward. It is very similar to the color of green being that it invokes feelings of hope and new growth. The color blue resonates with slowing down, self-esteem, relaxation and spirituality. If you want to lose weight, it is said to use blue plates when you eat because you will eat less and slow down.

Black – The color black resonates with spirituality, psychological and intellectual depth, wisdom and perspective. This color encourages thinking deeply, so great for an area of deep contemplation like the self-cultivation, knowledge or wisdom area of the Bagua map. However, it will invoke depression or lack of hope if used in excess. Use in small amounts in a room and don't overdo it.

Grey – The color grey is the marriage of white and black which signifies balance and the resolution of conflict. It is a color that resonates with transition and connection. It is a good color to use for the garage or to transition from the exterior to the interior space. Too much grey encourages hopelessness and frustration and resonates to the term, grey area.

Brown – The color brown resonates to a stable and well established foundation. However, it has a heavy feeling to it when it is used in excess. It carries the frequency of the passage of time and that something has existed for a long time. It symbolizes the wood element with depth and the season Autumn when things are generally in the decline phase.

Pink – The color of love and pure joy, compassion, happiness and romance. This is the color of the marriage and relationship area of the Bagua map and denotes hearts and fidelity.

Orange – The color of orange helps energy to become clearer. If uncovering emotions or facilitating communication with others is sought, orange will help promote this vibration. Orange is one of the colors used for caution or attraction, so it is excellent to use the color orange to get attention. It is also the color for security and fusion.

White – The color for a new start, purity, beginnings; white is the full spectrum of all colors. However, in the Chinese culture white is used for mourning. It represents the dead or dormant state. The Chinese avoid sleeping under a white blanket because it is similar to a burial shroud, however, white sheets are fine. If you love the color white and it is a good color for your environment then go ahead and use white in your environment. It also represents the metal element, so if you need additional metal in your Feng Shui design then the color white is a perfect choice to use for this cure in your home or office.

This concludes the colors of the Bagua map and their associated meanings, frequency and vibration. It is very important when experiencing the emotional pain of grief and loss to include colors in our environment that will lift us up and increase our vibration and frequency. It is important that you love the colors that you surround yourself with in your home environment. So take a moment after reading this chapter to look around your home and begin to notice some changes that you can make to your space that will increase your vibration and frequency so you will begin to love your environment and it will love you back.

I would like to add that you can look at your clothes in your closet and begin to notice what colors you wear on a regular basis. Do these clothes increase your vibrational frequency or are they taking away from your vibrancy. You can look at your wardrobe the same way as you look at your home environment and make some simple changes to increase your happiness quotient. Begin to use Feng Shui in your home or office environment and in your wardrobe and you will begin to see results in the way you look and feel. Enjoy the process and begin the journey to wholeness of mind, body and spirit through Feng Shui for healing grief and loss.

Feng Shui Checklist For Grief And Loss

This checklist is for you to use when you want to completely Feng Shui your home environment after experiencing grief or a loss in your life. I decided to end with this checklist because it will enable you to begin the process of letting go of the old and making way for the new beginning to appear in your life. It will show you the step by step process to making those changes easier for you.

Sometimes it is helpful to move to a new location or to a new home and these principles will still apply. In my life, it was very helpful for me to leave the old life completely and move forward to experience a new life. It was having faith and trust that I would be guided every step of the way by God and my angels. All I had to do was to be willing to make the change, be willing to let go of the pain and to let go of my old life. I made a choice that I wanted to be happy no matter what and then started taking the necessary action steps to move forward fearlessly in the direction of my desires and dreams and so can you. I've seen many other men and women do the same thing and take the courageous steps towards a better life.

Here is the checklist for you to use:

1. Clear the clutter and remove all those items in the home that you haven't used in one year or that no longer serve you or anyone else in your household. Only keep those things that you love and lift your vibration and spirit.

2. Do the space clearing of the entire space.

3. Align the Feng Shui Bagua Map to your home and determine where each sector falls within your home. You can create a drawing of your floor plan and then fill in the rooms and write in where the Bagua life sectors are located.

4. Determine the colors, shapes and body parts for each life area and write these inside each life sector on the floor plan.

5. Determine what Feng Shui cures and enhancements you would like to place in each life sector area. These can be what you already have in your home. These can also be new purchases that you make to reflect your new life. Write these on your floorplan.

6. Decide if you want to paint the walls, move furniture or buy new furniture for each life area.

7. Create an overall plan to consciously place items in each life sector area for a specific reason, paint the walls and move furniture.

8. Work the plan and make the necessary changes.

9. Watch your life shift and change as a result of your conscious efforts creating a home with peace, love and harmony.

10. Enjoy your new beginnings!

I am available if you would like help with this process. You can book a professional Feng Shui consultation with me by going to my website www.sandraruggles.com. When I do a professional consultation, I do a lot more than what I have listed above, but this process will get you started and on your way to making those changes that you desire to make for your new beginning. Congratulations on taking that next step forward towards a life of your dreams!

Conclusion

"The End" and a New Beginning...

> *"The End is where we start from"*
>
> —*T.S. Eliot*

As I write this conclusion to my book, I can't seem to get this old Beatles tune out of my head. The song, "The End", was recorded on my birthday, July 23, 1969 and is the perfect song for this conclusion and the end of my book. This was the last song recorded by all four of the Beatles for the album Abbey Road. This is "The End" of my book and the song I sing to all of you who I hope will heal quicker and easier than you ever imagined. If you listen to the words of the Beatles song, the basic meaning is that what you put into life is what you get out of life.

The same is true for this book that you have just read. If you complete the exercises and do the work, you will reap many rewards!

It is my wish for you that you will incorporate the exercises, tools and techniques into your everyday life as a conscious choice. You will find that your life will change for the better as a result.

When you make a decision to no longer feel like a victim in your life and look at every life experience and transition as a lesson with complete acceptance, you will find the peace within that you seek. There is no resistance to life when you have mastered complete acceptance and surrender. We may not be able to change what happens in our external world, but we do have control over our internal world and our response to the outside circumstances. This is the key to wholeness and staying centered throughout the storms we experience in life.

Forgiveness is a way to release anger and emotional pain. Forgiveness of yourself and others is so important in the healing process. The ability to forgive everyone and everything is the ultimate freedom in life. It can be hard to forgive yourself and others for those things in life we have experienced. However, when this is mastered, you will have complete peace and serenity. Isn't that what we all strive for in life? Living in the higher vibrations of love, peace, joy, compassion and serenity? You can have it all with the Power of Forgiveness. By following the Forgiveness process daily, weekly or monthly, you will begin to feel the difference in your life.

When you are ready to move through the stages of consciousness within your internal world, you are ready to begin the deep healing process of your soul. It is important to move beyond the ordinary consciousness of the five senses and include non-ordinary consciousness comprising imagination, creativity, dreams and intuition and incorporate these into your daily life. By moving to the higher levels of consciousness that connect you with God and the Divine energy of the Universe, you will begin to grow and connect with your "soul"utions through the non-ordinary consciousness. Spending time each day focusing on the higher levels of consciousness through meditation or prayer will allow you to connect with the Oneness of God and the Universe as you find peace, joy and love waiting for there.

In healing the mind to unlock the grief that has been encoded there by a change in your internal or external world, there is a six step process that you can implement into your life to begin the journey towards self-healing. These six steps will change the programming of your mind as you begin to think differently about your world and begin writing your new story. You will look at life through new eyes and see only what you wish to manifest into your world and release the past experiences that you no longer have control over in your life today.

In healing the Divine physical body, it is important to take into consideration the Tao which consists of the natural balance found in nature and the universal energies for natural healing found in the five elements of Wood, Fire, Earth, Metal and Water. When we achieve balance in our physical body using the five elements found in nature and the Universe at large, we are healthy and happy. We move through life in the flow of the natural rhythm and disease is less likely to occur when we are balanced. The body is the temple for the soul and that is why it is so important to consider it when healing our soul. A return to wholeness and balance can be achieved with the five elements and other physical remedies such as acupressure, acupuncture, essential oils, yoga and Wu Tao dance.

Aligning with Spirit is the next most important piece of the healing process to unlock the grief code. In this chapter, there are eight different ways to align with Spirit for your healing journey of the soul. If you incorporate just one or two into your daily life, you will find that these will be very effective in connecting with Spirit for healing. A few of these may already be a part of your life, so consider adding one or two that are not a part of your regular routine and you may experience a shift in all areas of your life as a result. Enjoy the journey towards wholeness as you embody Spirit.

After you unlock the grief code using the powerful mastery of acceptance, surrender, and forgiveness, you then begin to work on the mind, the body and the spirit with healing "soul"utions. At this point, you are ready for a new beginning and you are given a step by step process to customize your new lifestyle and write your new life story. Now you have the opportunity to create your personal roadmap to wholeness by creating by creating a calendar incorporating all the information you have received.

The final chapter in this book is dedicated to the Tao of healing using

Feng Shui principles for grief and loss. My book would not be complete without addressing the environment in which we live and work. This final chapter is a guide to creating an environment that is nurturing and one that feeds your soul on every level of your existence: mental, emotional, physical and spiritual. With the information from this chapter, you can begin to do your own basic Feng Shui of your home or office. This chapter includes simple steps to clearing the clutter, interior space clearing, color therapy, and a checklist with Feng Shui "soul"utions for grief and loss. It includes everything you need to heal your home or office environment.

I have now come to "The End" of this book. This is not really the end of anything because we all know whenever there is an ending there is always a new beginning ready to blossom. So for you my dear readers, I wish you well in your new beginning, now that you have Unlocked Your Grief Code!

Author Biography

Sandra is a Certified Life and Business Coach who specializes in grief recovery using holistic healing alternatives for mind, body and spirit. Sandra was given up for adoption at two days old and lived the life of an adopted child. This is a form of grief not often spoken about in our society but very real for adopted and foster children. Sandra lost her mother to breast cancer when she was 19. Two years later at 21, she became a widow and a single mother due to her husband's sudden death in a car accident. However, the final catalyst for writing this book came in 2009 due to a family estrangement with her two adult children.

She writes passionately and compassionately about her intense journey of the last four years using holistic practices, healing her cumulative grief. Sandra has been a holistic practitioner since 1997 and a Certified Life and Business Coach since 2007. She earned her B.S. Degree in Business Administration from California State University Sacramento and a Ph.D. in Esoteric Philosophy from the Ritberger Institute in California. Sandra has been a Certified Feng Shui Consultant since the year 2000 and includes Feng Shui as part of the healing process for grief and loss. Sandra is also Certified in Hypnosis and Neuro Linguistic Programming which she uses in her work. She studied at the Grief Coach Academy in Los Angeles in 2011 to receive specialized training in Grief Recovery Coaching for herself and now for others. Sandra is currently in the Practitioners training program at the Spiritual Center for Positive Living in Cameron Park, CA. Sandra currently resides in Northern California.

$100 Bonus Gift Included!

THE PATHWAY TO A PEACEFUL HEART -

HEALING RETREAT FOR GRIEF RECOVERY

This powerful and life-enriching Healing Retreat will offer participants an opportunity to learn new tools of self-discovery to move through and transform the emotional pain of grief and loss to an empowered life of deep peace, happiness, love and joy.

During the three day experiential Healing Retreat, you will learn new tools to change those thoughts, feelings, emotions, attitudes and beliefs that are keeping you "stuck" in the emotional pain of grief and loss. Grief is a normal reaction to loss that doesn't have to take years to recover. You will learn how to move through the grief and loss faster and easier than you ever thought possible leading to long-term recovery and a happier life.

Once you identify what is holding you back from living a life you love, you will take a step by step journey through many processes and techniques to eliminate what you no longer desire in your life and replace these things with a renewed sense of purpose, passion and peace. You will do this through holistic practices combining mind, body and spirit healing "soul"utions. The only true way to heal is through the mind, body, spirit connection which is not found in traditional grief recovery programs. You will then be ready to create your unique personal roadmap to wholeness and happiness and your Purpose, Passion and Pleasure Map. You will allow the new "you" to unfold and create a life you love.

Join a community of like-minded kindred spirits that will love and nurture you through this Retreat. Meet new friends that will love and support you for the rest of your life. You deserve to have a life you love.

For more information and to register for this Retreat go to: www.sandraruggles.com. Enter the code: LOVE to receive a 30% discount ($100.00 value). Bring a friend for FREE and join us for our next Healing Retreat.

Blessings,

Sandra